Study Guide

to accompany

Greaves • Zaller • Cannistraro • Murphey

CIVILIZATIONS OF THE WORLD: THE HUMAN ADVENTURE
Third Edition

Volume II: From the Middle 1600s

Richard L. Greaves
Robert O. Lawton Distinguished Professor of History
Florida State University

Robert Zaller
Professor of History
Drexel University

LONGMAN

An Imprint of Addison Wesley Longman, Inc

New York • Reading, Massachusetts • Menlo Park, California • Harlow, England
Don Mills, Ontario • Sydney • Mexico City • Madrid • Amsterdam

Study Guide to accompany Greaves, Zaller, Cannistraro and Murphey, *Civilizations of the World: The Human Adventure,* Third Edition, Volume II.

Copyright © 1997 Longman Publishers USA, a division of Addison Wesley Longman, Inc.

ISBN: 0-673-98343-9

97 98 99 00 01 9 8 7 6 5 4 3 2 1

CONTENTS

PREFACE

Perhaps more than any other subject in the academic curriculum, historical study provides a broad-ranging approach to human nature, political and social institutions, economic structures, intellectual and religious insights, and artistic achievements. Undertaken properly, historical study develops the ability, so essential to all modern careers, to gather factual data and to interpret it in a cogent, compelling manner. By understanding the past and how it developed and changed, we have a deeper appreciation of human achievements as well as an awareness of human failings. We become, then, more sensitive to the opportunities and needs of the present, both locally and internationally. The past is the key to the present, just as the present provides the foundation for the future. How we shape the present is conditioned by how we see the past.

Historical study, moreover, is the one academic discipline that is truly universal, for no subject is beyond the purview of the historian, whether it be the sciences, agriculture, music, literature, politics, gender relations, or food and clothing. The study of history thus provides the conceptual framework into which all of your college studies will fit. It is to enhance that process that this study guide has been prepared. Conscientious use of it will not only improve your academic performance but help to ensure that this course is one of the most meaningful of your college career.

USING THE GUIDE

Outline. Each chapter in this guide commences with an outline of the corresponding chapter to give you a sense of its organization, contents, and direction.

Overview. Study this summary before you read the corresponding chapter in the textbook, and reread it before you undertake the exercises that follow.

Geography. Most chapters in the guide have one or two outline maps to help you increase your knowledge of the world. Locate the places that are listed below each map, perhaps by using numbers. Then test yourself. Some chapters have short-answer questions on geographical topics to enhance your understanding.

Chronology. In history, as in your life, it is important to know the order in which events have happened. Use this section to help you remember how the pieces of the past fit together. The answers are found at the end of the chapter exercises in this guide.

Identification. Every discipline, including history, demands a knowledge of the basic facts before you can apply or interpret them. Use this section to develop a mastery of many of the important facts in the chapter. To identify these items, indicate who or what they were; when and where they lived or happened; and why they were important.

Definition. These are terms you need to know in order to communicate about the subjects in the chapter. Define them as carefully as possible.

Completion. This section will provide a quick check to determine how well you understood the chapter and the previous exercises. The answers are found at the end of the guide.

Short Answer. Having established a basic mastery of the facts, you are now ready to function as a historian by interpreting the data. In answering each question, reexamine the pertinent facts and then formulate your own conclusion.

Understanding the Documents. Historians work mostly from "primary sources," that is, the actual records of the period under examination. Selections of such documents are provided in the text. In this section you will have an opportunity to analyze them yourself.

Points to Ponder. In every period of history significant developments have occurred which are relevant to that and later ages. Observations about such developments are sometimes controversial or even contradictory. The "points" provided here are intended to focus your attention on such developments. They are especially useful as starting points for group discussions.

Term-Paper Topics. In a subject as vast as the history of world civilizations, possible subjects for research are legion. The topics suggested here have been chosen with an eye to their appropriateness for the typical 15 to 20 page paper, as well as for breadth of interest. In preparing any of these topics, make an effort to use primary sources as well as works by modern historians.

CHAPTER 21

THE TRANSFORMATION OF AFRICA, 1400-1800

OUTLINE

OVERVIEW

In the 400 years between 1400 and 1800, Africa changed significantly. Socially and economically, the major changes involved (1) the spread of craft guilds that were closed to outsiders and resembled castes, especially in the western Sudan; (2) the growth of predatory economies in the African states bordering the Mediterranean and Indian Ocean, where pirates operated with relative impunity, disrupting trade and impeding economic and technological development; (3) the rise of a trading-post economy in western Africa, where the Portuguese served as middlemen, tending to exclude Africans from the prosperous merchant class; (4) an alteration in the pattern of landholding, especially in North Africa, Ethiopia, and the western Sudan, where landowners encouraged the growth of tenant farming, and in central Africa, where pastoralists provided cattle and land to farmers in return for labor; and (5) the decline of the *jonya* system, in which captives owned most of what they produced and could not be bought or sold, and its gradual replacement by slaveholding as it was practiced in the lands of the eastern Mediterranean.

Important changes also occurred in religion, with the continuing spread of Islam into eastern Ethiopia and the empire of Songhay. Christianity lost some ground to Islam in Ethiopia and missionary efforts in West Africa were largely unsuccessful, but large numbers of converts were won in Kongo owing to the incorporation of traditional beliefs and customs as well as the work of such prophetesses as Doña Beatrice Kimpa Vita.

In the political realm this period witnessed the Ottoman conquest of North Africa; the rise of such new states as Songhay, Oyo, and Dahomey; and the centralization of others, such as Benin and Kongo. In the Sudan, Songhay became a powerful state under the rule of Sonni Ali (1464-1492) and Muhammad Touré (1493-1528), both of whom were Muslims (though Sonni Ali's commitment has been questioned). Both men not only expanded the empire but also developed its bureaucracy, and Muhammad founded a professional army of slave soldiers. The Yoruba people of Oyo established a powerful empire in the eighteenth century in what is now Nigeria, conducting business with Arabs to the north and supplying slaves for the transatlantic trade. The rulers of Dahomey also provided slaves for that commerce, some of whom were their own criminals and others were acquired from inland sources. Benin, located in the area of the Niger River delta, reached the peak of its power between 1450 and 1650, when its rulers, or *obas*, presided over a centralized government. The masterful artists of Benin were apparently indebted to the earlier Nok culture. Kongo's rulers increased their power by encouraging the spread of Christianity, thereby undercutting traditional religious leaders.

In both Kongo and Ethiopia, migratory groups—the Jaga and the Oromo respectively—weakened existing states. The same fate befell the Swahili city-states, which had already been suppressed to some degree by the Portuguese, as the Zimba, a Bantu group, moved through the region in the late sixteenth century. In South Africa, migrants from Great Zimbabwe, whose trade had declined and whose soil was depleted, moved northeastward to found the Mutapa state in the mid-fifteenth century. As another Bantu group, the Nguni, migrated southward, they confronted the Dutch, with whom the first hostilities began in 1702.

Perhaps no change was more dramatic than the commencement of the transatlantic slave trade in the sixteenth century. In the ensuing centuries, between 9 and 12 million Africans were shipped to the Americas. Assante and Dahomey prospered because of this traffic in humans, but most African states gained little. The slave trade predated its transatlantic phase, but the cumulative impact on African society and politics was destructive, with entire family groups, clans, and villages wiped out.

The transatlantic trade did result in the introduction to Africa of such new foods as maize, cassava, sweet potatoes, beans, tomatoes, onions, pumpkins, and red peppers as well as pigs. Despite its relatively low nutritional value, the cassava became an important element in the African diet. Other new foods, including peas, broad beans, and lentils, came to Africa from the Middle East. So great was the impact of cassava and maize by 1850 that some historians argue that Africa experienced an agricultural revolution in this period.

POINTS TO PONDER

1. "Islam came to West Africa as a merchants' religion and was identified with commerce from the start." (Philip Curtin)

2. Christianity attracted many converts in Kongo by adapting to traditional African religious beliefs and practices.

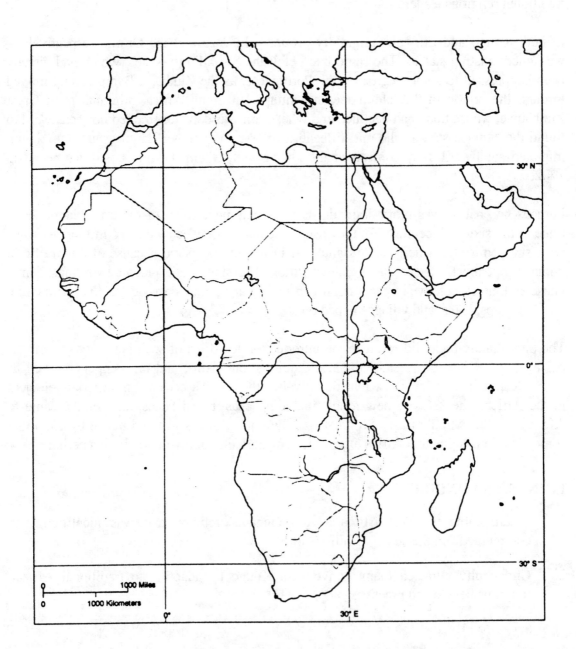

GEOGRAPHY

Locate the following on the map:

Sudan	Senegambia
Ethiopia	Kongo
Songhay	Angola
Kanem-Bornu	Kilwa
Hausa states	Zanzibar
Benin	Great Zimbabwe
Oyo	Mutapa
Dahomey	Kalahari Desert

CHRONOLOGY

1. _____ Arrival of the Portuguese in the Indian Ocean

2. _____ Reign of Idris Aloma in Kanem-Bornu

3. _____ Rule of Sonni Ali in Songhay

4. _____ Abandonment of Great Zimbabwe

5. _____ *Marabout* movement

6. _____ Afonso I embraces Christianity in Kongo

7. _____ British occupy the Cape

IDENTIFICATION

1. Lebna Dengel

2. Oromo

3. Songhay

4. Sonni Ali

5. Muhammad Touré

6. Idris Aloma

7. Yoruba

8. *Marabout* movement

9. Afonso I

10. Mutapa empire

11. Nguni

12. Tsonga

DEFINITION

1. *Jonya* system

2. *Signares*

3. Entrepôt

4. Maghreb

5. Cassava

6. *Alafin*

COMPLETION

1. The predatory economy developed in the African states bordering the

    _____ and _____ Ocean.

2. The native African form of captivity was known as the _____.

3. The unique Christianity of _____ was a blend of

    Coptic, Old Testament, and Judaic elements.

4. Songhay became a major empire during the rule of _____.

5. Oyo society was organized by seniority rather than _____.

6. The *marabout* movement, which opposed the overseas slave trade, was launched by

    the western _____ in the seventeenth century.

7. The African and Eurafrican women of Senegal who amassed substantial wealth and

    became an important economic, social, and cultural link between Africans and

    Europeans were called _____.

8. Doña Beatrice Kimpa Vita blended traditional African and _____

    beliefs in her teachings.

9. Kilwa, Sofala, and Mozambique were _____ city-states.

10. The Mutapa state was founded in the mid-fifteenth century by migrants from

    _____.

11. Although the slave trade generally did not substantially benefit the African economy, the West African states of _____ and _____ were exceptions.

SHORT ANSWER

1. How did the *jonya* system differ from eastern Mediterannean slavery?

2. What were the characteristic features of the predatory economy in North Africa?

3. How did the entrepôt economy of West Africa affect the Africans of that region?

4. What impact did warfare between Christians and Muslims have on Ethiopia?

5. What powers did the *alafin* of Oyo possess?

6. Why were the *signares* important?

7. Why was Christianity accepted by many people in Kongo?

8.   Why was Kilwa's location a key to its economic success?

9.   How did the slave trade in Africa change after 1500?

10.   What was the impact of the slave trade on African women?

11.   What was the effect of the introduction of maize and cassava in Africa?

UNDERSTANDING THE DOCUMENTS

1.   What does the account of Islam's introduction to Kano suggest about the reception of this religion in sub-Saharan Africa?

2.   Why did the Rev. John Lindsay find African women so admirable?

3.   What does the European visitor's description of Kilwa in the early sixteenth century tell us about life in this city?

4.   How would the life of the Nguni differ from that of the residents of Kilwa?

5.   Judging from the early eighteenth-century account of a Dutch West India Company official, assess the impact of the slave trade on the people of West Africa.

TERM-PAPER TOPICS

The *Signares*
The *Marabout* Movement
Ethiopian Christianity
Christian Missions in Kongo
The Empire of Songhay
The African Travels of Leo Africanus
Idris Aloma: Islamic Ruler
Benin City
Gender in Oyo Society
Slavery in Sub-Saharan Africa Before c. 1600
The Rise of the Transatlantic Slave Trade
The Role of Oyo and Dahomey in the Slave Trade
The Introduction of New Foods to Africa
Nguni Culture
The Zimba and the Jaga
Swahili Culture
Sonni Ali and the Rise of Songhay
The Predatory Economy of North Africa
The *Jonya* System

CHAPTER 22

IMPERIAL REVIVAL IN CHINA

OUTLINE

OVERVIEW

As Mongol power in China weakened in the early fourteenth century, banditry and revolt erupted until, in the 1350s and 1360s, the rebel leader Chu Yuan-chang (Dzu Yuan-zhang) established control and founded the Ming dynasty. Before its demise in 1644, the Ming rebuilt the empire and ushered in an era of unprecedented economic and cultural development. Under their rule, population probably increased by at least 50 percent, the number and size of cities grew, and trade may have doubled. The Ming also expanded the traditional tributary system, which eventually embraced more than forty states from Korea and Japan to the Philippines. Between 1405 and 1503, Admiral Cheng Ho (Zhenghe) launched seven mammoth naval expeditions that ranged as far as Arabia and East Africa, seeking tribute and new trade opportunities.

Agriculture was still regarded as the basic source of wealth, and new crops, such as maize and potatoes, were introduced as a result of trade with the Philippines. Although commerce was officially frowned upon, the Ming period witnessed major commercial growth, thanks in part to the silver that paid for China's exports of tea, silk, porcelain, and other goods. In fact, in the early sixteenth century, capital investment began shifting from land to trade and manufacturing, leading to a demand for new technology, such as mechanical looms. Guilds of money changers and bankers grew in importance as well.

The arts and literature flourished, encouraged by the patronage of merchants. The second Ming emperor, Yung-lo (Yongluo), commissioned an enormous encyclopedia to which 3,000 scholars contributed. Novels, which were invented in Asia, were popular reading; among the best known were *Water Margins*, the story of an outlaw band, and *The Golden Lotus*, a satire about the amorous life of a druggist. The theater, puppet shows, and opera flourished as forms of popular entertainment, often centering on themes sympathetic to the powerless, especially women. Elite culture tended to be very conservative, as reflected in the "eight-legged essay" required of candidates in the imperial examination system. Schools stressed the Confucian message of responsibility and "human-heartedness." The center of elite culture was Peking (Beijing), the new imperial capital, which was designed to reflect imperial power and majesty. The city, laid out according to astronomical principles, was intended to impress visitors.

By the sixteenth century, the Ming had become complacent and were slow to learn from visiting Europeans. Administrative effectiveness declined, factions maneuvered for power, and the weaker emperors had a greater affinity for pleasure than government. Inflation weakened the economy, and corruption and bribery were rampant. Even the army became increasingly ineffective, despite the fact that it had doubled in size in the Ming era; the quality of recruits dropped sharply and Chinese weapons were inferior to those of their enemies, including the Japanese. Once again, banditry and social revolt were on the rise. Finally, in 1644 a Ming general requested aid from the Manchus, who had by this point adopted Chinese culture, to defeat a bandit force in Peking. The Manchus agreed, and in the course of the next four decades extended their domination throughout all of China, establishing the Ch'ing (Qing) dynasty.

POINTS TO PONDER

1. "The Chinese saw their interests best served by further embellishing their home base rather than by pursuing less rewarding foreign contacts."

2. While the Ming rulers maintained order and administered justice almost to the end, their increasing conservatism prevented them from responding to the need for change.

3. "The normal Chinese government is essentially based on moral force; it is not a despotism." (T. T. Meadows, 1856)

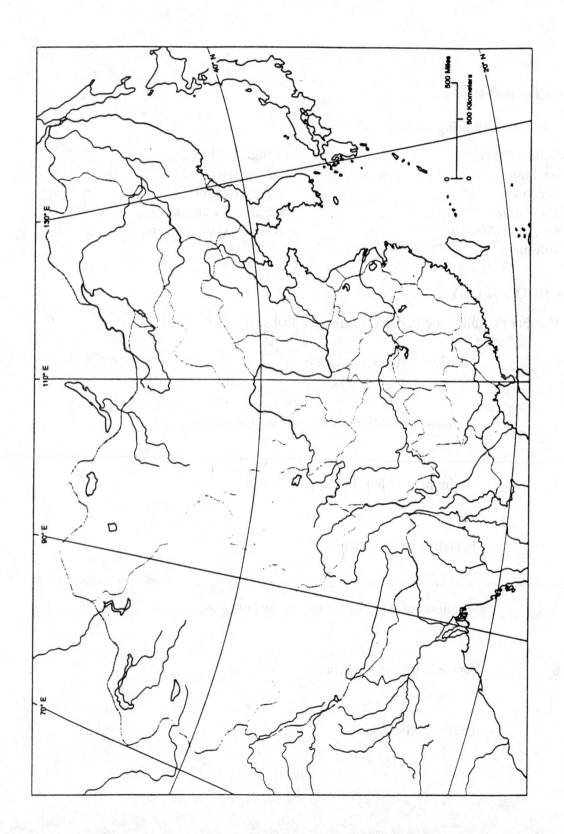

GEOGRAPHY

Locate the following on the map:

Yellow River
Nanking
Sinkiang
Manchuria
Szechuan (Sichuan)
Taiwan

Yangtze valley
Peking (Beijing)
Inner Mongolia
Canton (Kwangzhou)
Hsiang (Xiang) River

CHRONOLOGY

Number the following in correct chronological sequence:

1. _____ First Jesuit mission to China

2. _____ Maritime expeditions of Cheng Ho (Zhenghe)

3. _____ Beginning of Manchu conquest of China

4. _____ Founding of Ming dynasty

5. _____ Abolition of Imperial Secretariat by Hung-wu

6. _____ Japanese invasion of Korea

7. _____ Death of Nurhachi

IDENTIFICATION

1. White Lotus
2. Hung-wu
3. Yung-lo (Yongluo)
4. Cheng Ho (Zhenghe)
5. *The Golden Lotus*
6. *Water Margins*
7. Chang Chu-cheng (Zhang Juzheng)
8. Tung Lin (Donglin)
9. Wan-li
10. Li Tzu-ch'eng (Li Zicheng)
11. Nurhachi

DEFINITION

1. Ming dynasty

2. K'e t'ou ("kowtow")

3. Tributary system

4. Ch'ing (Qing) dynasty

COMPLETION

1. The first Ming emperor was the intelligent, strong-willed _____.

2. The _____ system required foreign states to acknowledge Chinese greatness and cultural superiority.

3. The naval expeditions of _____ sailed as far as India, the Persian Gulf, and East Africa.

4. In the Ming Empire the predominant fabric for the clothing of the common people was _____.

5. In the sixteenth century China acquired much of its silver through favorable balances of trade with _____ and _____.

6. The enormous Ming encyclopedia was commissioned by _____.

7. Perhaps the two most popular Ming novels were _____ and _____.

8. Most Ming scholars were interested in upholding _____.

9. The Forbidden City was part of the city of _____.

10. The first Europeans to arrive in China in the early 1500s were the _____ and the _____.

11. Before launching their invasion of China in 1644, the Manchus conquered _____ and _____.

SHORT ANSWER

1. What were conditions like in China on the eve of the founding of the Ming dynasty?

2. What were the goals and accomplishments of Hung-wu?

3. What was the purpose of the tributary system?

4. Why did Cheng Ho (Zhenghe) mount his naval expeditions, and what did they accomplish?

5. What were the effects of the strong conservative outlook in Ming China?

6. What were the principal characteristics of the Ming economy?

7. What were the major technological achievements of Ming China?

8. What were some of the dominant themes of Ming novels, and what do they suggest about society in this period?

9. Compare elite and popular culture in the Ming period.

10. Compare Peking (Beijing) under the Ming with contemporary Istanbul.

11. What factors account for the decline of the Ming dynasty? Could its fall have been prevented?

UNDERSTANDING THE DOCUMENTS

1. How did the Chinese view Cheng Ho's expeditions?

2. What picture of Chinese society emerges from the journals of Matteo Ricci?

3. What do the maxims and the interpretation of the 1626 earthquake indicate about Chinese values and the Chinese outlook on life?

TERM-PAPER TOPICS

The Image of Chinese Society in *The Golden Lotus* and *Water Margins*
China as Seen by European Visitors in the Sixteenth Century
Peasant Rebellions in the Late Ming Period
Peking in the Sixteenth Century
The Expeditions of Cheng Ho
The White Lotus
Hung-wu, the Rebel Emperor
The Expansion of the Tributary System in Ming China
Trading Patterns in Ming China
Popular Culture in the Ming Age
Chinese Folk Art in the Ming Period
The Jesuits in China
Ming Porcelain
The Decline of the Ming Empire
The "Eight-Legged Essay" and the Ideal of Conservatism

CHAPTER 23

THE SOCIETIES OF THE EARLY MODERN WORLD

OUTLINE

Social Hierarchies
    Caste and the Social Order in India
    Social Hierarchy in East Asia
    Social Hierarchy in Europe
    The European Aristocracy
    Urban Society
Marriage and the Family
    The Family in Asia
    The Family in Europe
    Marriage in Asia
    Divorce in Asia and Europe
    Marriage and the Family in Africa
The Status of Women
    Women in Asia
    Women in the Middle East and Africa
    Women in Europe
Sexual Customs
Education, Literacy, and the Printed Word
    Learning in Asia
    Learning in the West
    Education in the Ottoman Empire
Poverty, Crime, and Social Control
    Causes of European Poverty
    Poor Relief in Europe
    Poor Relief Outside Europe
    Crime and Poverty
    Controlling Crime

OVERVIEW

In both Asia and Europe, hierarchy was fundamental to social structure. Generally, Asians acquired status through learning, a characteristic that tended to distinguish them from most other societies. The system of caste was uniquely Indian and evolved as a way to structure a society that had been plagued by chronic disruption. The essence of caste was ritual purity and pollution, and it operated largely in terms of subcastes, or *jatis*, each of which was normally tied to a particular occupation. In the rest of Asia, apart from distinctly Buddhist and Muslim areas, status was determined by power and responsibility, and in China by merit, as determined by the system of imperial examinations. Europeans structured their societies according to estates, or social groups defined by degrees of fixed status. Birth was more important than wealth, but the source of one's wealth was also significant; landed wealth was more prestigious than commercial profit. Asians and Europeans alike accepted the principle that status entailed responsibility.

Hierarchy was also fundamental to family structure, and in both Asia and Europe the family's welfare took precedence over the individual. Filial obedience and a sense of collective responsibility were basic to the Asian family. Among the European aristocracy this was also generally true, at least until the sixteenth century, but among lower estates the conjugal family was probably the norm. Among the upper social orders, the European family began to change about the middle of the sixteenth century as more importance was attached to the nuclear core and the sense of kin responsibility declined.

The arranged marriage was common among the European aristocracy and at all levels in Asian society. In contrast, the Incas allowed state officials rather than the family to arrange marriages for those slow to act on their own. Polygamy was practiced by the Muslims, the Aztecs, the Incas, and many African tribes. Divorce was possible in Asia, though rare, but not in Europe until the Protestant Reformation; in Catholic lands, however, annulments could be obtained if specific conditions were satisfied.

In nearly every early modern society, women were subordinate to men. Asian widows, for instance, were not allowed to remarry, although Asian women played an important role in shaping family life. Islamic women were urged to confine their activities to the home and were rarely educated or allowed to engage in commerce. A few West African tribes accorded women virtually equal status, and in some cases they served as chiefs. Europeans tended to think of women as bearers of children, sexual partners, and social companions,

22

although at the lower levels of society wives were in practice virtually partners with their husbands in the quest to make a living. At the upper levels, some women acquired an education and became writers, translators, or painters.

Some Asian and African societies linked sex and religious ritual, but women as a rule were expected to be chaste, as in the West. Catholicism stressed that intercourse should only be for procreation, but some Protestant leaders began to accept sexual pleasure in marriage as a legitimate manifestation of love. Birth-control was generally frowned on by both Catholic and Protestant leaders, but was openly discussed in health manuals, as were methods of inducing abortion. Christians and Muslims officially condemned homosexuality, although its practice probably caused less concern in Islamic lands.

Asians in general may have had a greater respect for learning than people of other societies, especially since education was the principal path to success. In early modern Europe, there was an increase in literacy and schools, as well as the continued development of univer-sities. Protestants and Catholics alike looked to the latter to provide leaders. Jews everywhere gave strong support to learning, but the Ottoman Turks limited education to those who were affluent or politically powerful.

Poverty was common throughout early modern Europe, especially because of population growth and periodic harvest failures. Western governments generally relied on coercion to keep the destitute from flooding into the cities. Some places established workhouses and prohibited begging, as also happened in the coastal towns of West Africa. Care for the needy among the Incas was undertaken by the government, which apportioned land to families based on their size; the state also stockpiled food in the event of future shortfalls. In Asia the wider family was the principal source of poor relief, and the Chinese, like the Incas, tried stockpiling in the "ever–normal granary system." Muslims used their mandatory tax, the *zakat*, to fund institutions that aided the needy.

Most criminal activity in the early modern world was caused by poverty. As the latter increased, so did theft and banditry. European governments responded by reorganizing the personnel and procedures to control crime. In Asia and Europe alike, the system of justice was designed to develop a sense of awe in the accused, and punishments were intended as deterrents, hence public displays of convicted criminals were commonplace.

POINTS TO PONDER

1.   The numerous parallels in the history of early modern societies underscore the commonness of human experience.

2.   Religious beliefs played a major role in shaping the way early modern people viewed their respective societies.

3.   "All the inequality which now prevails owes its strength and growth to the development of our faculties and the advance of the human mind, and becomes at last permanent and legitimate by the establishment of property and laws." (Jean Jacques Rousseau, 1755)

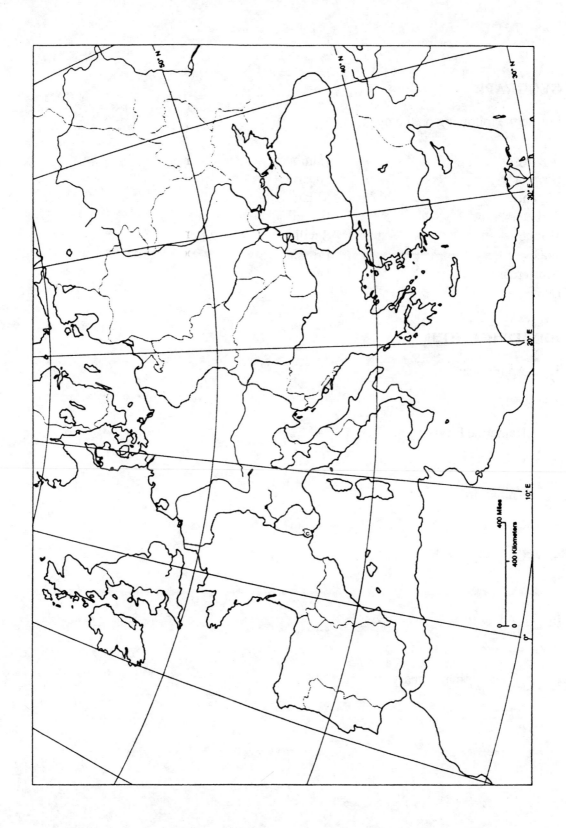

GEOGRAPHY

Locate the following on the map:

Saxony   Hamburg
Bavaria   Austria
Florence   Milan
St. Petersburg Berlin
Venice   Seville
Wales   Prussia
Amsterdam   Genoa
Lyons

IDENTIFICATION

1. Aphra Behn

2. Katherine Boyle

3. Kamasutra

4. Lady Murasaki

5. Oratory of Jesus

6. "Ever–normal granary system"

DEFINITION

1. Caste

2. Jati

3. Sanskritization

4. Estates

5. Patricians

6. Purdah

7. Nuclear family

8. Sati

9. Infanticide

10. *Coitus reservatus*

11. *Coitus interruptus*

12. Shaming

13. Medreses

14. "Fur-collar criminals"

15. Picaresque novel

16. "Drawing and quartering"

COMPLETION

1. Asian civilizations placed a heavy emphasis on seeking status and advancement through _____.

2. The essence of caste is _____ and _____.

3. In Europe, society was largely shaped by _____, that is, social groups defined by degrees of fixed status.

4. The Asian family was hierarchical in structure, with absolute power vested in the _____.

5. During the early modern period in Europe, the decline of kinship was accompanied by the growing importance of the _____ family.

6. The Catholic Church allowed the annulment of a marriage in specific circumstances but prohibited _____ in the modern sense.

7. The basic unit of social organization in sub-Saharan Africa was _____.

8. Most African women were accorded a subordinate social role, but in _____ the "dual-sex" system allotted them much greater status.

9. The Catholic Church regarded _____ as the primary purpose of sexual intercourse.

10. In the West, universal education first began in _____.

11. Higher education in the Ottoman Empire was provided in theological schools known

    as _____.

12. The most common form of crime in early modern Europe was _____.

SHORT ANSWER

1. How did the caste system operate?

2. How was the social hierarchy in Europe structured?

3. Why did many European aristocrats have problems in the early modern period?

4. What role did the family play in Asian society?

5. How did the family change in Europe in the early modern era?

6. What factors did Asians consider with respect to marriage?

7. How was divorce viewed in Asia and Europe?

8. How were marriage and the family viewed in sub-Saharan Africa?

9. Did women fare better in Asia than in the Middle East or Africa?

10. What was the status of women in early modern Europe?

11. What considerations governed sexual relations in Asia and Europe?

12. Did Asians accord greater respect to learning than Europeans and Ottoman Turks?

13. What were the major forms of poor relief in the various early modern societies? Were any effective?

14. What was the relationship between poverty and crime?

UNDERSTANDING THE DOCUMENTS

1. What does the 1615 decree about the *daimyo* and the *samurai* reveal about the importance of hierarchy in Japan?

2. What does the European practice of disposing of "surplus" daughters suggest about the status of women and the role of the church?

3. Were wives more valued in India than in the West?

4. Were the conditions of the poor in early modern France worse than that of the poor today?

5. Was property more important to Europeans than human life?

TERM-PAPER TOPICS

The Caste System in India
The Practice of *Sati* in India
The Practice of Infanticide in Early Modern Europe
Techniques for Birth Control in the Early Modern World
"Fur-collar" Crime in Europe
The East Asian Family in the Early Modern Era
The Arranged Marriage in Early Modern Europe
Divorce in Asia and Europe
Marriage Customs in Sub-Saharan Africa
The Status of Women in Early Modern Europe and East Asia: A Comparison
The Status of Women in West African Tribes in the Pre-Colonial Period
The *Geisha* Tradition in Japan
Sexual Behavior as Outlined in the *Kamasutra*
Prostitution in Early Modern Europe
Literacy in Europe and Asia: A Comparative Study
Education in the Ottoman Empire, c. 1600-c. 1800
Attitudes Toward the Poor in Europe, West Africa, and Asia
The Punishment of Criminals in Europe and Asia in the Early Modern Period

CHAPTER 24

THE AGE OF ABSOLUTISM

OUTLINE

OVERVIEW

The European nation-state was consolidated in the seventeenth and eighteenth centuries. Because this consolidation was achieved largely through the efforts of monarchs and their bureaucracies in the name of absolute power, this period is commonly known as the age of absolutism. Absolute power was justified through the principle of divine right, which asserted that monarchs held their titles directly from God and were accountable only to him for their actions on earth. Absolute power was not arbitrary, for rulers were meant to govern wisely and beneficently. Whether they did so however was not for their subjects to judge, and those who resisted a divinely-appointed ruler were held to be in peril of damnation.

The absolute monarchs used their power to centralize their authority, stripping provincial magnates and representative assemblies of their independence. To strengthen the national economy they attacked local privileges and exemptions, established and directed new industries, established overseas colonies and exerted control over trade and finance. To finance these policies, collectively called mercantilism, they imposed direct taxes. To compete with their fellow sovereigns, they built standing armies. The ultimate purpose of this activity was to achieve what the French called *gloire*. *Gloire* was a combination of wealth, prestige, and honor; it belonged both to the nation and to the ruler. It was won in many ways, but chiefly through battle. For this reason, conflict was the norm of international conduct, and peace was regarded merely as a recuperative interval between wars.

In general, those states which succeeded in achieving stable centralization, including Britain and Prussia, were better able to lay claim to internal resources, achieve sustained growth, and compete in an international arena whose material stakes were increasingly significant. Those states which, though larger, were more diffuse, such as Austria and Russia, were relatively less successful, and prone to often paralyzing civil disturbances. The case of France, whose wealth and dynastic ambition made it the leading Continental power of the period, showed the limits of a central authority that imposed itself on the traditional elite without conciliating it. Louis XIV, the greatest ruler of the age, was able to extend the powers of the French monarchy far beyond any of his predecessors and to dominate European politics for more than fifty years, but at his death the nobility regained much of its power, and its continuing conflict with the throne was a prime cause of the Revolution of 1789.

In contrast, in Britain, where monarchy seemed to have sustained a grave defeat in the Glorious Revolution of 1688, the domination of an aristocratic and merchant elite produced a state at once more flexible and more unified than anything achieved on the Continent. As these episodes show, divine right absolutism was often vigorously challenged, and modern democratic theory was in large part forged through resistance to it.

The efforts at state-building had profound effects on the institutions and orders of society. In Britain, the needs of the state created a modern system of credit and finance and laid the foundations of empire, while in France the demands of warfare, combined with bad harvests, caused famines of unprecedented scope. In Prussia, the militarization of society produced a population that, disciplined at all levels, achieved impressive growth, but at the same time shaped habits of obedience that impeded the growth of genuine civil institutions. In parts of Prussia and Austria as well as the whole of Russia, the peasantry fell into serfdom, a process which had severe consequences for social and economic development; in contrast, the development of a free labor market in Britain helped to create an aggressively commercial economy. At the same time, however, the state's achievements made it the target of demands by aristocrats seeking to exercise its power, merchants seeking its protection and favor, workers demanding support for their living standards, and peasants seeking relief from taxes and traditional obligations.

POINTS TO PONDER

1.   The consolidation of state power in–seventeenth and eighteenth–century Europe was largely the result of divine right absolutism, although Britain accomplished it by overthrowing absolute monarchy.

2.   War was considered the natural state of affairs in this period, and national prestige was reckoned by conquest.

3.   The building of state power profoundly affected all other institutions of society.

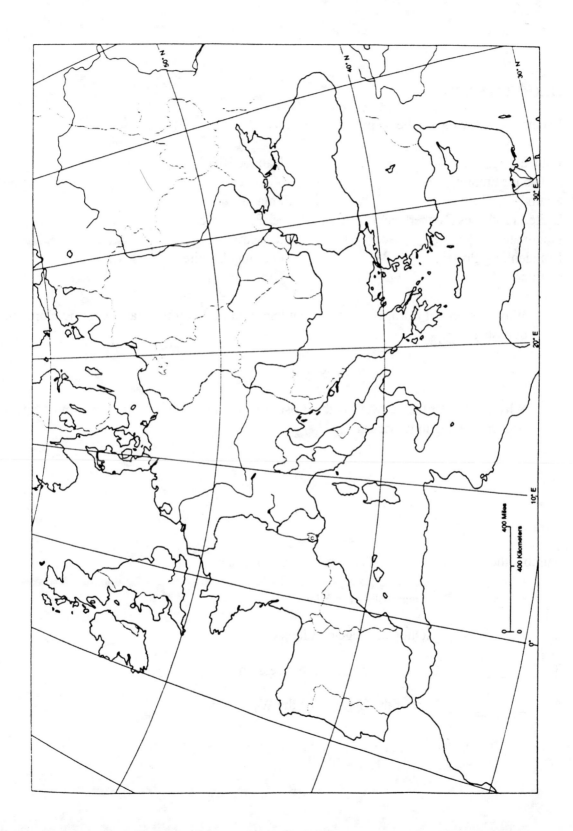

GEOGRAPHY

Locate the following on the map:

France	Danube River
Habsburg Empire	Vienna
Spain	Poland
United Provinces (Netherlands)	St. Petersburg
Palatinate	Moscow
Brandenburg-Prussia	Ottoman Empire
Germany	Gibraltar

1. Why was central Europe so often a battleground between the Habsburg and Bourbon dynasties?

2. Why did the British as well as the Austrians feel that Bourbon domination of Spain was threatening to its security?

CHRONOLOGY

Number the following in correct chronological sequence:

1. _____ Death of Louis XIV

2. _____ Ottoman siege of Vienna

3. _____ War of the Spanish Succession

4. _____ Peter the Great visits the West

5. _____ Establishment of the Prussian General Directory

6. _____ Peace of Utrecht

7. _____ Glorious Revolution in England

8. _____ League of Augsburg

9. _____ Treaty of Nystadt

IDENTIFICATION

1. St. Petersburg

2. Bill of Rights

3. Jean-Baptiste Colbert

4. Pragmatic Sanction

5. *Intendants*

6. William of Orange

7. Treaty of Karlowitz

8. Jan Sobieski

9. Bank of England

10. *Ulozhenie*

11. Magyars

12. Versailles

13. Table of Ranks

14. Charles II of Spain

15. Mark of Brandenburg

DEFINITION

1. Divine Right

2. Glorious Revolution

3. Pragmatic Sanction

4. *Gloire*

5. Test Act

6. *Gabelle*

7. Hohenzollern Dynasty

8. Stadholder

COMPLETION

1. The two parties who emerged in England in support of and opposition to the Stuart

   dynasty were the _____.

2. The small number of ministers who served Louis XIV were in marked contrast to the

   size of his bloated state _____.

3. To control religion, Peter the Great placed the Russian Orthodox Church under the

   control of a state body, the _____.

4. The key to Prussia's military success was the maintenance of a _____.

5. The most influential woman in France during the later decades of Louis XIV's reign was _____.

6. A weakness of the Austrian empire was the continual agitation for independence on the part of _____.

7. The first elected Parliament that sat in England after the Restoration was known as the _____ because of its intense royalism.

8. Russia emerged as a major European power as a result of the conflict with _____ known as the _____.

9. The Nine Years' War and the War of the Spanish Succession were both fought to contain the power of _____.

10. The first great ruler of Brandenburg-Prussia was popularly known as _____.

SHORT ANSWER

1. Why did England accept a foreign conqueror in the person of William of Orange?

2. How was the power of Peter the Great different from that of other European monarchs?

3. Why was the great French famine of 1694-1695 a manmade disaster?

4. How did the Bank of England help England finance its wars?

5. Why was the death of Charles II of Spain the occasion of a European crisis?

6. Why did Charles VI of Austria feel it necessary to win diplomatic support for Maria Theresa's accession to the Habsburg throne?

7. What were the basic features of the Revolutionary Settlement in England?

8. How did the other states of Europe react to Russia's emergence as a major power?

9. In what ways was civilian life in Prussia affected by the presence of the army?

10. In what ways was the changing character of urban life in Europe revealed by the example of London?

UNDERSTANDING THE DOCUMENTS

1. How does Bishop Bossuet exalt royal power by comparing it to divine power?

2. How does Fénelon define the responsibilities of a king and why does he feel that Louis XIV has failed to discharge them?

3. What does Pososhkov's complaint reveal about the state of justice in Russia and the power of its nobility and its judges over ordinary subjects?

4. How does Locke justify the right of rebellion against unjust rule?

TERM-PAPER TOPICS

Divine Right in Theory and Practice
The Court of Louis XIV
The Dutch Republic in the Seventeenth Century
Madame de Maintenon
The Spanish Succession Crisis
Peter the Great
The Rise of Prussia
The First Age of Global War
The Role of Warfare in European State-Building
The Rise of Serfdom in Eastern Europe
The Glorious Revolution
John Locke and the Resistance to Absolute Monarchy
London in the Age of Hogarth

CHAPTER 25

THE CENTURY OF GENIUS

OUTLINE

From Ancient Science to the Copernican Revolution
      The Legacy of Antiquity
      The Medieval World Picture
      The Hermetic Challenge
The New Order of Knowledge
      Galileo and the Copernican Triumph
      Other Scientific Advances
      New Technology
Science at the Crossroads
      Doubt and Faith: Descartes and Pascal
      Conflicting Roads to Truth
      The Newtonian Synthesis
      The Scientific Method
Philosophy: The Age of Reason
      Thomas Hobbes and the Natural Man
      John Locke and the State of Nature
      French Skepticism
      The Lens Grinder of Amsterdam, Baruch Spinoza
Literature: The Triumph of the Vernacular
The Age of the Baroque
      Rome: The Rebirth of a Capital

OVERVIEW

The Scientific Revolution offered the West a new way of describing the physical world, and a new standard of truth. Hitherto, the highest form of knowledge had been communicated through divine revelation and contained in sacred texts. What was true about the created world and what was necessary to faith and morals was already known. Because that truth was held to be certain and immutable, great weight was given to tradition and authority— not merely to the sacred texts themselves, notably the Bible, but to the commentaries and interpretations of the early church fathers and the institutional church. All other forms of knowledge derived from observation and reason were subordinate to the knowledge given by revelation. Where the two conflicted, revealed or religious knowledge necessarily prevailed.

The rational and empirical tradition was nonetheless older than the revealed one, with roots far back in pre-Christian antiquity. In addition, certain forms of occult and mystical knowledge, particularly Neoplatonism, had survived from antiquity. These traditions were resumed in the Middle Ages and converged during the Renaissance, leading both to a revival of speculation about the physical world and to the practice of occult and magical arts. At the same time, the Protestant Reformation sharply challenged the traditional interpretations of religious truth and the authority of the Catholic church.

The Scientific Revolution began with the publication in 1543 of Copernicus' theory that the sun rather than the earth was the center of the universe. Copernicus was a devout Christian, but he based his theory on observation, mathematical reasoning, and Neoplatonic speculation rather than accepted belief. Because the Copernican theory conflicted with traditional religious interpretations based on the geocentric or earth-centered theory, it caused great controversy for more than a century until it was generally accepted. During that period, scientists such as Galileo and Kepler and philosophers such as Bruno, Bacon, and Descartes extended our knowledge of the physical universe and evolved new standards of demonstration and proof. The scientific method, based on careful observation, deductive logic, and mathematical reasoning, was finally perfected by Sir Isaac Newton, who described the entire cosmos in terms of three laws of motion.

The nature of scientific understanding, based upon principles of trial and error, served both to call accepted traditions of knowledge into question and to suggest that all knowledge, new and old, must submit itself to the scrutiny of reason. The consequences of this were felt in religion, philosophy, and the arts. For both René Descartes and Blaise Pascal, the new science opened an intolerable abyss in the world, casting faith as well as knowledge in doubt. Descartes reacted by affirming the primacy of reason in reaching certain knowledge, while Pascal, despairing of the intellect, turned to faith as the only guarantee of salvation. In contrast, Thomas Hobbes described a social world ruled by passion and interest, whereas John Locke argued for a society that was, like reason itself, self-correcting. In literature, the questioning of received knowledge was linked to a dethronement of Latin, the language of tradition, in favor of the vernacular. The result was to stimulate new literary traditions in England, France, Germany, the Netherlands, and Spain, while a brilliant new style, the baroque, flourished in music and the classic arts. Finally, the Bible itself was subjected to a scrutiny designed to purge it of inconsistencies and errors, and the philosopher Spinoza urged that reason be accepted as a guide to moral as well as natural knowledge.

POINTS TO PONDER

1. The Scientific Revolution challenged traditional forms of knowledge based on faith and authority.

2. The Scientific Revolution evolved a new standard of proof based on observation and reasoning.

3. The effects of the Scientific Revolution were strongly felt in philosophy, politics, and the arts.

CHRONOLOGY

Number the following in correct chronological sequence:

1. _____ Galileo's discovery of Jupiter's moons

2. _____ Newton's *Mathematical Principles of Natural Philosophy*

3. _____ Giordano Bruno burned at the stake

4. _____ Closing of the London stage

5. _____ Ptolemaic theory of the universe

6. _____ Harvey discovers the circulation of the blood

7. _____ Copernicus' *On the Revolution of the Heavenly Spheres*

8. _____ Founding of the Royal Society

9. _____ Simon's *Critical History of the New Testament*

IDENTIFICATION

1. Hermes Trismegistus

2. *Dialogue Concerning the Two Chief World Systems*

3. Johannes Kepler

4. Molière

5. Paracelsus

6. Heliocentric theory

7. State of nature

8. Baruch Spinoza

9. *Paradise Lost*

10. Cartesianism

11. John Locke

12. Baroque

13. François Rabelais

14. Tycho Brahe

15. Royal Society

16. Sor Juana

DEFINITION

1. Copernican theory

2. Jansenism

3. *Leviathan*

4. Hermeticism

5. Vernacular literature

6. Scientific method

7. Quintessence

8. Pascal's wager

COMPLETION

1. The deductive method in science was championed by the English philosopher

   _____.

2. Galileo discovered the moons of Jupiter with the aid of a newly invented instrument,

   _____.

3. The legacy of ancient science was preserved during the Dark Ages by

   _____.

4. "A war of all against all" describes _____ theory of man in

   the state of nature.

5. The problem of plotting straight-line courses on two-dimensional maps was solved by

   _____.

6. "I think, therefore I am" was the starting-point of the philosophy of _____.

7. The first modern novel was Miguel de Cervantes' _____.

8. The heliocentric theory was first put forward by the ancient Greek scientist

   _____.

9. The greatest musician of the German baroque was _____.

10. The key to Newton's system was the principle of _____.

SHORT ANSWER

1. What flaws in the geocentric theory led Copernicus to reject it?

2. What was the influence of Neoplatonism on the development of the Scientific Revolution?

3. Why was Galileo's discovery of Jupiter's moons significant?

4. Why was Giordano Bruno judged to be a heretic by the Catholic church?

5. How did John Locke's view of the state of nature differ from that of Thomas Hobbes?

6. Why was mathematics of crucial importance to the Scientific Revolution?

7. How were the needs of technology instrumental in promoting the Scientific Revolution?

8. What led to the rise of skepticism in the seventeenth century?

9. Why was Latin increasingly replaced by vernacular languages as an instrument of expression in the seventeenth century?

10. How did the English, French, and Spanish theaters reflect the values of their respective societies in the seventeenth century?

UNDERSTANDING THE DOCUMENTS

1. How did Giordano Bruno's theory of an infinite universe affect contemporary scientific and religious thinking?

2. How were both the ideas of Bacon and Descartes important to the development of the scientific method?

3. How do Thomas Hobbes and Gerrard Winstanley differ in their account of the origins of civil society?

TERM-PAPER TOPICS

Ancient and Medieval Science
The Hermetic Tradition and the Scientific Revolution
The Reaction to Copernican Theory in the Sixteenth and Seventeenth Centuries
Giordano Bruno: Martyr of the New Science
Galileo: Discoverer of the Heavens
The Rise of Skepticism
The Development of the Scientific Method
The First Scientific Societies
Sir Isaac Newton: The Scientist as Hero
Pascal's Quest for Faith
Hobbes and Locke on Civil Society
Spinoza, the Lonely Heretic
The Baroque Style in the Arts
The Golden Age of Theater
Women Writers of the Seventeenth Century
Sor Juana and the Struggle for Literary Freedom
Rome: The Rebirth of a City

CHAPTER 26

EUROPE AND THE AMERICAS

OUTLINE

OVERVIEW

The eighteenth century saw the development of a worldwide economy for the first time in history. Its center was in Europe and particularly in the empires of Britain and France, which competed on four continents for dominance throughout the period. In some parts of the world, notably Asia, this economy was still peripheral, but Europe, Africa, and the Americas were united through conquest, colonization, and commerce in a network of migration, resource transfer, and trade in raw and finished products known as the Old Colonial System.

At the beginning of the century, the largest empire in the New World was still that of Spain, which covered most of central and South America with the major exception of Portuguese Brazil. Both Spain and Portugal had declined as European powers, however, and Britain particularly had made inroads on the Spanish colonial economy by treaty, backdoor trade, and smuggling. Britain's own empire was centered in the sugar islands of the Caribbean and the settler colonies of the North Atlantic seaboard, while the French, in addition to their own sugar islands, had staked out large areas of Canada and the Mississippi valley.

During the first two centuries of settlement, the New World had been chiefly valued as a source of the gold and silver bullion that played such a vital role in the expansion of the European economy. By the eighteenth century, its primary focus was on the production of plantation crops, including sugar, tobacco, and coffee, for which there was an enormous demand in Europe. This trade involved Africa as a supplier of slave labor, and millions of black Africans crossed the Atlantic during the eighteenth century and much of the nineteenth to create the wealth on which the Western economy relied. The inhuman conditions under which the slaves were both transported and worked eventually resulted in movements to abolish first the slave trade and then slavery itself. Despite the formal renunciation of both by most European powers in the early nineteenth century, slavery was only eliminated in the United States as a result of the Civil War, and persisted even longer in Cuba and Brazil.

The Old Colonial System was finally broken up by the series of revolutions that began with the rebellion of the thirteen colonies in 1775 and ended about 1825 with the liberation of Mexico, Central America, and South America. In part this breakup was caused by the maturing of certain colonial economies, notably that of the United States; in part from the decreased economic importance of the New World that resulted from the exhaustion of the

South American mines, the debility of Spain, and the collapse of the sugar market; and in part from the example of European revolutions themselves. It produced a future world power in the United States of America; the beginnings of dominion in Canada; and the establishment of a multitude of mostly Spanish-speaking states in Central and South America that continue, for the most part, to search for political stability, social reform, and sustainable growth to the present day. For Britain, the loss of the thirteen colonies coincided with its conquest of the state of Bengal and the beginning of its domination over India, and thus the arrival of European empire on the continent of Asia.

Within Europe itself, the early modern economy saw an increasing differentiation between the market-oriented economies of the West and the peasant-based ones of the East, with the latter assuming the role of agricultural supplier and enserfing much of its peasantry. The political and economic center of gravity shifted toward the Atlantic in the eighteenth century with the rise of British and French power. Britain's constitutional settlement and the consolidation of its elite produced the most stable as well as the most commercially successful state in Europe, and laid the groundwork for the Industrial Revolution. At the same time, Europe's wars of empire, now global in scope, made for shifting alliances and a fluid balance of power within which intense interstate rivalry took place. Not until the cycle of imperial wars that lasted from 1689 to 1815 ended did the powers begin their search for a mechanism by which direct conflicts between them could be avoided.

POINTS TO PONDER

1. The eighteenth century saw the development of the first global economy, based principally on Europe, the Western Hemisphere, and Africa, but with Asia playing a role of increasing significance as well.

2. Britain and France superseded Spain and Portugal as the major imperial powers in the New World in the eighteenth century, as a plantation economy based on slavery replaced one based on the export of bullion.

3. The market-based economies of western Europe achieved domination not only of their colonial economies but of those of eastern Europe as well.

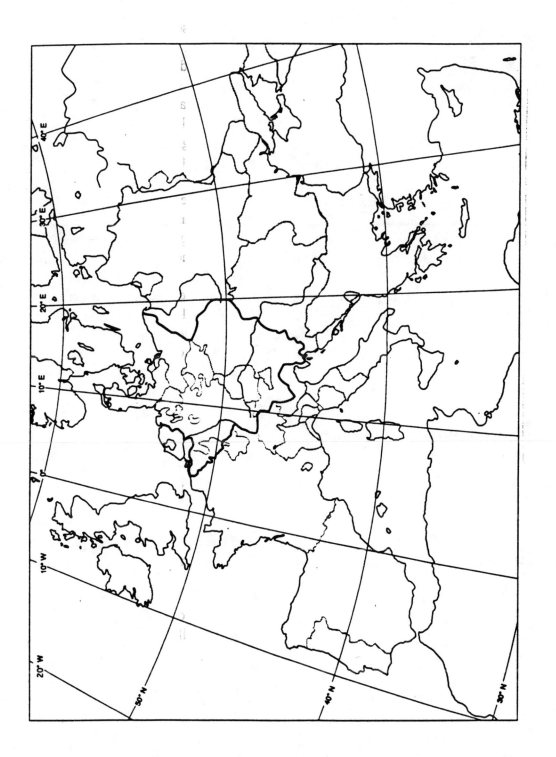

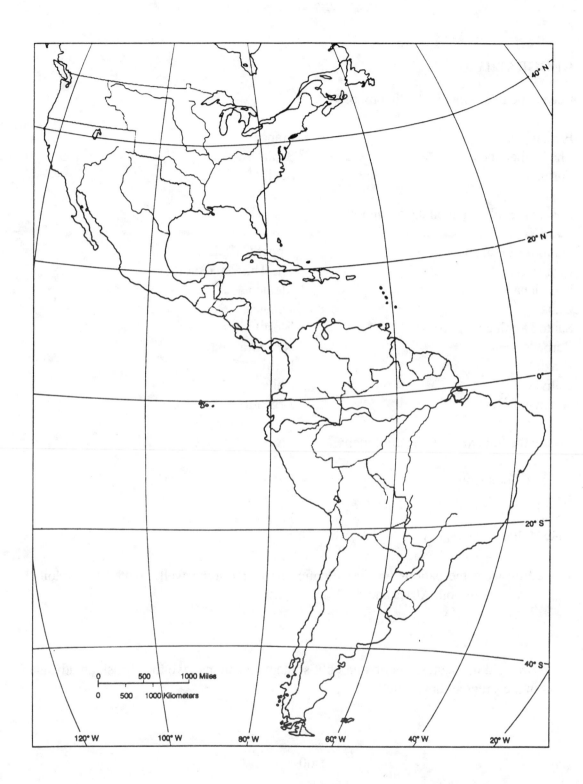

GEOGRAPHY

Locate the following on the first map:

British Isles	France
The Netherlands	Spain
Portugal	Seville

Locate the following on the second map:

Isthmus of Panama	Upper Canada
Lower Canada	The Thirteen Colonies
Louisiana Purchase	Mexico
Cuba	Jamaica
Santo Domingo (Haiti)	West Indies
Barbados	New Granada
Brazil	Peru
Bolivia	Chile
Amazon River	Argentina

Locate the following on the third map:

Cape of Good Hope	India
Bengal	Gold Coast
Ceylon	East India
New Holland (Australia)	

1. Why were the nations on the Atlantic coast of Europe well situated to exploit the resources of both Africa and the New World?

2. How did the acquisition of small but strategic locations give the British an advantage in the struggle for empire?

CHRONOLOGY

Number the following in correct chronological sequence:

1. _____ Fall of Quebec

2. _____ British acquire Jamaica

3. _____ Collapse of the South Sea and Mississippi Companies

4. _____ Battle of Plassey

5. _____ Revolt of the thirteen colonies

6. _____ Spanish conquest of the West Indies

7. _____ French driven from Haiti

8. _____ Death of Simón Bolívar

9. _____ Walpole Prime Minister in Britain

IDENTIFICATION

1. Merchant capitalism

2. Plantation society

3. Navigation Acts

4.	Middle Passage

5.	Sir Robert Walpole

6.	John Law

7.	Sons of Liberty

8.	Pragmatic Sanction

9.	Louis XV

10.	Articles of Confederation

11.	Tecumseh

12.	Adam Smith

13. Northwest Ordinance

14. Simón Bolívar

15. José de San Martín

DEFINITION

1. Mercantilism

2. Triangular trade

3. Ministerial responsibility

4. Enclosure

5. Metropolis

6. Old Colonial System

7.   Manifest Destiny

8.   Devolution

COMPLETION

1.   In the seventeenth century, Europe's economic center of gravity shifted for the first

      time away from _____.

2.   The primary factor in the growth of a worldwide economy in the sixteenth and

      seventeenth centuries was the transportation of _____

      from the New World.

3.   The first slave-based plantation economy in the New World was   developed in

      _____.

4.   The chief European port for the sugar and slave trade was _____.

5.   The statesman who rallied Britain during the Seven Years' War was _____.

6.   American colonists were angered when the Canadian frontier was   extended to the

      Ohio River by the _____.

7. Upper and Lower Canada were reunited following recommendations made by the

_____.

8. Adam Smith argued in *The Wealth of Nations* that the Old Colonial System be

replaced by a system of _____.

9. The chief architect and spokesman of the American constitution was

_____.

10. Simón Bolívar was nicknamed _____.

SHORT ANSWER

1. How did the slave trade stimulate the creation of a global economy?

2. How did the expansion of the early modern state stimulate the growth of merchant capitalism?

3. How did the British and the French differ in their approach to colonial settlement in North America?

4. Why was the slave trade necessary to replenish the slave population of the Americas?

5. How did the social and political position of the English aristocracy differ from that of Continental aristocracies?

6. Why were the British unable to retain control of the thirteen colonies despite superior land and naval forces?

7. What were the defects of the Articles of Confederation?

8. What factors led to the abolition of the slave trade by most European nations in the early nineteenth century?

9. Why were Spain's former colonies unable to form stable societies after winning their independence?

10. How did the struggle for empire affect the traditional balance of power in the eighteenth century?

UNDERSTANDING THE DOCUMENTS

1. How does Espinosa's account of illegal labor conscription in New Spain illustrate the limits of Spanish colonial authority in the New World?

2. What does Equiano's description of his experience on a slave ship suggest about the reciprocal attitudes of whites and blacks toward each other?

3. How does Chetwood's account of the South Sea Bubble suggest the emergence of a commercial mentality in eighteenth-century Britain that cut across all classes?

4. Why did Bolívar, in leading the South American revolutions, feel they would be unable to produce stable and cohesive societies?

TERM-PAPER TOPICS

The Old Colonial System
Bullion and the Expansion of Europe
The Beginnings of a Global Economy
Mercantilism in Theory and Practice
Sugar and the Slave Trade
Slavery and Society in the New World
The Balance of Power: Myth or Reality?
The South Sea Bubble
The Beginnings of British India
The Struggle for North America
The Loss of the Thirteen Colonies
Manifest Destiny: Visions of Empire in the Early American Republic
Alexis de Tocqueville's View of America
The Abolition of the Slave Trade
Bolívar and the Lost Revolution

CHAPTER 27

THE ENLIGHTENMENT

OUTLINE

OVERVIEW

The Enlightenment was a wide-ranging critique of the social and intellectual bases of eighteenth-century culture. Unlike other movements of renewal and reform since the advent of Christianity, the Enlightenment was not based upon religious revival but was stimulated by the Scientific Revolution. The thought of the Enlightenment was secular and rationalist, and this, in a society where art, science, political authority, and morality had acknowledged the primacy of religious truth for 1500 years posed a revolutionary challenge to the social order.

At the same time, the Enlightenment was also a response to economic and political changes at work in European society. Many of its most influential figures, or *philosophes*, were of bourgeois origin. Unattached to church or court, they appealed directly to the public that the new literacy had created. In their quest for freedom and toleration, their conception of a worldwide human community, and their contempt for inherited privilege, they echoed the demands of an emerging commercial society for free trade, unfettered enterprise, and an expanding global economy.

The *philosophes'* chief hope for the achievement of their goals rested with the enlightened despots. These rulers, notably Frederick the Great of Prussia, Catherine the Great of Russia, and Joseph II of Austria, searching for a basis of authority beyond divine right, professed their desire to govern according to Enlightenment principles. Only Joseph made a genuine attempt to do so, however, and his efforts were frustrated and ultimately reversed. Nonetheless, the broadest political principle of the Enlightenment—equality before the law for all persons—continued to stimulate movements to incorporate those previously excluded from citizenship, including Jews, women, and colonial slaves. These movements resulted in the abolition of the slave trade and the emancipation of the Jews, and the beginnings of modern feminism.

The Enlightenment ideal of progress and rationality engendered its own reaction, the Counter-Enlightenment. This movement emphasized the cultivation of individuality and personal sentiment, and was characterized by a revival of religious feeling and expression. It thus marked the onset of the dominant cultural trend of the next century, Romanticism.

POINTS TO PONDER

1. The Enlightenment derived its emphasis on rationality from the Scientific Revolution and on the needs of an emerging commercial society.

2. The *philosophes* sought to realize their goals through sympathetic rulers, the enlightened despots.

3. The Enlightenment resulted in significant reforms, including the abolition of the slave trade, the emancipation of the Jews, and the beginnings of women's liberation.

CHRONOLOGY

Number the following in correct chronological sequence:

1. _____ First volume of the *Encyclopedia* published

2. _____ Pugachev's Rebellion

3. _____ Reforms of Joseph II

4. _____ John Wesley begins his ministry

5. _____ Abolition of the slave trade

6. _____ Debate between the Ancients and the Moderns

7. _____ Rousseau's *Social Contract*

8. _____ Sabbatai Zevi attempts to lead the Jews to Palestine

9. _____ French Protestants regain freedom of worship

IDENTIFICATION

1.   Philosophe

2.   Deism

3.   Ancients and Moderns

4.   John Locke

5.   Voltaire

6.   Rousseau

7.   Montesquieu

8.   Encyclopedia

9.   Court Jews

10. Pietism

11. Journal des Dames

12. Mary Wollstonecraft

13. Joseph II

14. Immanuel Kant

15. Samuel Johnson

DEFINITION

1. Enlightened Despotism

2. General Will

3. Hasidism

4.   Rococo

5.   Counter-Enlightenment

6.   Great Chain of Being

7.   Methodism

8.   Social Contract

COMPLETION

1.   In *An Essay on Toleration*, _____ declared that all

    religions were worthy of respect.

2.   The notion that all social, political, and even moral problems could be solved by

    human effort gave rise to the doctrine of _____.

3.   _____ was greatly influenced by the freedom of English

    institutions and Newtonian thought.

4.   Rousseau found the origin of social injustice in the institution of _____.

5.   A separation of the powers of government was advocated by _____.

6.   "I am the first servant of the state" was the statement of _____.

7. An important movement for reform within the Anglican church was

    _____ _____.

8. Lessing made a Jewish philosopher the hero of his play _____.

9. The center of the European musical world in the late eighteenth and early nineteenth

    century was _____.

10. The first ruler to abolish serfdom and judicial torture was _____.

SHORT ANSWER

1. How did the *philosophes* attempt to evade censorship?

2. How did Locke's view of the mind as a blank slate differ from that of Christian orthodoxy?

3. Why did Catherine the Great's Legislative Commission fail to produce a genuine reform of the Russian legal code?

4. How did Frederick the Great's practice differ from his professed Enlightenment principles?

5. Why was Joseph II unsuccessful in attempting to implement his reforms?

6. Why was the reform of children's education a principal objective of the Enlightenment?

7. What were the disabilities under which the Jews of Europe lived prior to emancipation?

8. Why did feminist writers of the eighteenth century wish to reform the institution of marriage?

9. How was the expansion of literacy reflected in the new literary forms of the eighteenth century?

10. How does the career of a composer such as Beethoven illustrate the new freedom of the creative artist in the early nineteenth century?

UNDERSTANDING THE DOCUMENTS

1. How does Diderot invoke the idea of progress in calling upon posterity to judge the merits of his *Encyclopedia*?

2. How does Frederick the Great justify the idea of absolute rule on the basis of an appeal to the general welfare?

3. How does Blake use the image of sand to show the vanity of human reason? What does he mean in this poem by "Israel"?

4. What reaction does the author of this passage from a letter of 1778 want us to have to the scene he is describing? How did he select his details to achieve the effect he desired? What does his own attitude toward the blacks appear to be?

TERM-PAPER TOPICS

The Great Chain of Being
Deism and the God of Reason
Locke and Liberty
Voltaire: The First *Philosophe*
Rousseau and the Idea of the Social Contract
Diderot and His *Encyclopedia*
Censorship and the Enlightenment
The Enlightened Despots
Joseph II: Tragic Reformer
The Counter-Enlightenment and the Revival of Religion
Sense and Sensibility: The New Reading Public of the Eighteenth Century
The Emancipation of the Jews
Mary Wollstonecraft: Pioneer Feminist
The Golden Age of Viennese Music

CHAPTER 28

THE FRENCH REVOLUTION AND NAPOLEON

OUTLINE

OVERVIEW

The French Revolution of 1789 swept aside a political and social order that had stood in France for nearly 1,000 years. Within a few months, it overturned the system of orders that had been the basis of French society for centuries, and challenged the Old Regime everywhere in Europe. It proceeded to overthrow the monarchy, creating a republic based on the idea of civil equality, and spawning satellite states in the Netherlands, Switzerland, and Italy by conquest despite the armed opposition of most of the major powers of Europe. Proclaiming its mission to liberate oppressed peoples, it carried its message around the world, profoundly affecting revolutionary movements from its own day to ours. From the very beginning, contemporaries recognized it as the most important event of the age. Two centuries later, historians are still debating its meaning and impact.

The outbreak of revolution in 1789 may be traced to a combination of chronic fiscal insolvency, an aristocratic insurrection against a weakened throne, and growing demands for representative government.

At first, it was focused on efforts to create a constitutional monarchy. These efforts foundered for a number of reasons. By sweeping away the privileged orders on which the monarchy had rested, it reduced King Louis XVI to a figurehead. The emigration of the nobility and the alienation of the church created a counterrevolutionary interest that fomented internal dissent and external hostility to the new regime. This in turn generated sentiment for a republic and enthusiasm for a war of liberation, which broke out in 1792.

Louis' arrest and execution and the proclamation of a republic released a surge of popular energy, as witnessed by the success of the revolutionary armies; it also polarized the nation still further. Civil war, foreign threat, and the pressure of the highly politicized masses of Paris led to a radical dictatorship whose goals were lost in a repression that appeared as it gathered momentum to become an end in itself. After the overthrow of this government and its leader, Maximilien Robespierre, a succession of regimes sought to consolidate power and achieve stability. Finally, a military coup paved the way for the dictatorship of Napoleon Bonaparte.

Napoleon presented himself as the true heir of the revolution; what he did was to define it in terms of a pseudo-monarchical autocracy, which paid lip service to revolutionary principles while denying them political expression. His conquests, which at their height brought half of Europe directly or indirectly under his rule, brought his version of the revolution to much of the Continent, where it played an important role in stimulating German and Italian nationalism. His wars also brought to an end the cycle of imperial struggles with Britain that had begun in 1689, and to the French domination of the Continent that dated back to Louis XIV. The personal empire he had sought to create crumbled with his fall, and the general alliance that had defeated him restored the Bourbon monarchy to France.

Despite this apparent setback, the revolution had lasting consequences. It defined if it did not achieve democratic citizenship, and it placed the issues of representative government and social justice on the agenda of European politics. It also provided, under Robespierre's Terror, a matrix for modern totalitarian government. The socialist, liberal, and Fascist politics of the next two centuries would all in some degree trace their pedigree back to the French Revolution.

POINTS TO PONDER

1. The French Revolution challenged the fundamental bases of Old Regime society and sought to replace them with a new ideal of community.

2. The Revolution set the agenda for nineteenth-century politics and the model for both liberal and totalitarian societies in Europe.

3. The Revolution ended in the military dictatorship of Napoleon, but Napoleon's conquests helped spread some of its basic principles around the globe.

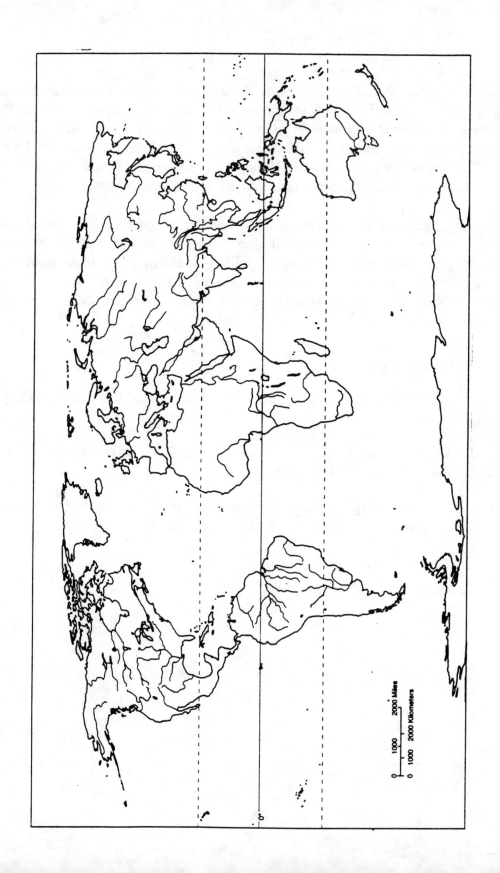

2000 Miles

1000

2000 Kilometers

1000

0   1000

GEOGRAPHY

Locate the following on the map:

Paris	Grand Duchy of Warsaw
Berlin	Austrian Empire
Lyons	Vienna
Corsica	Austerlitz
Spain	Moscow
Cape Trafalgar	St. Petersburg
Prussia	

1. How did the lack of a strong power to the north and east of France help explain the success of the revolutionary armies?

2. How did the vast distances of Russia frustrate and ultimately defeat Napoleon's Grand Army in the campaign of 1812?

CHRONOLOGY

Number the following in correct chronological sequence:

1. _____ Execution of Louis XVI

2. _____ Battle of Austerlitz

3. _____ Reform of the parlements by Maupeou

4. _____ Ninth of Thermidor; fall of Robespierre

5. _____ Promulgation of the Napoleonic Code

6. _____ Declaration of the Rights of Man and the Citizen

7. _____ Napoleon's invasion of Russia

8. _____ Civil Constitution of the Clergy

9. _____ Treaty of Campo Formio

IDENTIFICATION

1. Assembly of Notables

2. Third Estate

3. National Convention

4. Declaration of the Rights of Man and the Citizen

5. Assignats

6. Madame Roland

7. September Massacres

8. Committee of Public Safety

9. Reign of Terror

10. Directory

11. Abbé Sieyès

12. Consulate

13. Talleyrand

14. Treaty of Tilsit

15. Battle of the Nations

DEFINITION

1. Sans-culottes

2. Passive citizens

3. Guillotine

4. Thermidorian Reaction

5. Manifesto of the Equals

6. Continental System

7. Volksgeist

8. Hundred Days

COMPLETION

1. The body that was convened by Louis XVI in 1789 was _____.

2. The wave of popular hysteria that gripped France in the wake of the storming of the Bastille was known as _____.

3. The most powerful attack on the Revolution of 1789 was *Reflections on the Revolution in France* by _____.

4. The dominant social group in the Constituent Assembly and its legislative successors was the _____.

5. Prussia and Austria pledged themselves to the restoration of the French monarchy in the _____.

6. The spontaneous unions of municipal councils and provincial militias that sprang up in support of the Revolution were known as the _____.

7. The two major political groupings in the National Convention were the _____ and the _____.

8. The general conscription ordered by the National Convention in the summer of 1793 was known as the _____.

9. The coup of the Eighteenth of Brumaire brought _____ to power in France.

10. Napoleon's dream of conquering Britain was destroyed at the naval battle of

_____.

11. Napoleon was exiled after his abdication to the island of _____, and,

after his defeat at the Battle of Waterloo, to the remoter island of _____.

SHORT ANSWER

1. How did the fiscal crisis of France contribute to the outbreak of the French Revolution?

2. Why was the Constitution of 1791 unable to resolve the role of the executive in the new government?

3. Why did the attempt to retire the public debt through the sale of church lands and the use of assignats prove a failure?

4. What were the factors that led to the surprising success of the revolutionary armies in 1792-1793?

5. How was the judicial process perverted during the Terror?

6. Why was the Directory unable to establish itself firmly?

7. How did Napoleon transform the revolutionary republic into an empire ruled by himself?

8. How did Napoleon succeed in resolving the conflict with the Catholic church and reconciling it to his rule?

9. What were the effects of Napoleon's conquests on Germany, Italy, and Spain?

10. Why was France treated leniently after its defeat by the Allied coalition?

UNDERSTANDING THE DOCUMENTS

1. What were the major circumstances that led Arthur Young to expect a revolution in France? To what extent was his analysis borne out by subsequent events?

2. What does Humbert's account of the storming of the Bastille reveal about the temper of the revolutionary crowd in Paris and the state of royal authority?

3. How did Olympe de Gouges appeal to the Enlightenment belief in the laws of nature in asserting her claim for female equality?

4.   How does Robespierre define a revolutionary government? How in his view does it differ from a constitutional government?

5.   How does Napoleon understand the principles of majority rule and popular sovereignty? Is his conception of them compatible with a genuine belief in democratic government?

TERM-PAPER TOPICS

Interpreting the French Revolution
The Influence of the American Revolution on the Revolution of 1789
The Fall of the French Monarchy
The Third Estate and the Bourgeoisie
The Meaning of Citizenship in the French Revolution
Women in the French Revolution
The Counter-Revolution
European Reactions to the French Revolution
The Role of the *Sans-Culottes*
The Life of Robespierre
The Meaning of the Terror
Gracchus Babeuf and the Conspiracy of the Equals
Napoleon's Rise to Power
The European Resistance to Napoleon
Napoleon in Russia: The Fatal Campaign

GLOBAL ESSAY

DEATH AND THE HUMAN EXPERIENCE (II)

OVERVIEW

Funerary practices and attitudes toward death reflect both wide variation among different cultures and a common goal: that of integrating the most universal of all human experiences with the needs of the living community. The deceased have usually been regarded as entering a different plane of existence, for which elaborate preparations were often necessary. These included ritual purifications designed both to assist the deceased and to protect the living. The major world religions have believed that the fate of the deceased reflects his or her conduct while living. Death itself has been interpreted both as a release from earthly sorrow and as a punishment for sin. Formal bereavement may last a year or more, and memorial services, as in Buddhist folk practice, can be required for up to nearly half a century.

Funeral customs have often been affected by cultural interchange. This has been the case particularly since the coming of Western colonialism to most of the globe. Not only did Western missionaries and officials seek to convert native populations to Christianity, but to eradicate practices they regarded as heathen and offensive. French Jesuits attempted to stop the Huron Indian custom of killing and eating war captives, and the British to suppress *sati* or widow suicide in India. Often local priests or shamans bitterly resisted Western intrusion, blaming any subsequent misfortunes on the community's departure from correct custom.

Within cultures, funeral practices have often evolved. Western society has encompassed a wide variety of attitudes toward death since the Reformation, which broke the Catholic church's monopoly on dogma and ritual. Baroque playwrights and artists of the seventeenth century often emphasized the erotic element in death, while the Enlightenment saw the replacement of church burials with interment in public cemeteries, a practice that both distanced the dead from the living and underscored the need to recognize the individuality of the deceased by a separate space and memorial that became family property. The nineteenth century, with its emphasis on emotional sincerity, encouraged public expressions of grief, but the present age has depersonalized mourning, in many cases to the point of near denial. No doubt future custom will continue to reflect broad cultural trends.

IDENTIFICATION

1.   Trial of the Grave

2.   Kami

3.   Bhakti Movement

4.   *Sati*

5.   Feast of Courage

6.   Feast of the Dead

7.   Husein

8.   Kiddush Hashem

COMPLETION

1. The angelic interrogators of the soul in Islam are _____ and

   _____.

2. According to Buddhist folk belief, death occurs when _____

   _____.

3. A de–emphasis on death ritual was characteristic of the _____

   in Europe and the _____ in India.

4. Suicide committed at holy places was considered a sacred act by _____

   and _____.

5. Exhumation and reburial of the dead was a vital part of the culture of the

   _____.

6. As many Christians symbolically reenact the death of Jesus at Easter, so Muslims

   annually commemorate the death of _____.

7. The raising of funeral monuments and public statues to famous individuals was

   characteristic of Western culture in the _____.

8. The belief that martyrdom was a sanctification of God's name was a comfort to many

   _____ during World War II.

SHORT ANSWER

1. What are some of the ways in which folk custom and religion have sought to lessen the fear of death?

2. In what ways do African myths about the origin of death resemble traditional Judeo-Christian explanations?

3. How did popular beliefs in the powers of the dead cause conflict with Western missionaries trying to alter burial customs?

4. Why did Huron culture disintegrate when the tribe was moved from its ancestral ground by authorities?

5. How did religious suicide by Buddhist monks affect the course of the Vietnam War?

6. How was death associated with sensual pleasure and eroticism in the seventeenth-century West?

7. Why did World War I bring about a sharp alteration in attitudes toward death in the West?

TERM-PAPER TOPICS

The Muslim Conception of the Afterlife
Reforming Death: Protestant and Bhakti Attitudes During the Early Modern Era
The Origin of Death in African Mythology
Death Ritual in Modern China
Death and the Enlightenment
Death and the Victorians
The American Way of Death
Jewish Responses to the Holocaust

CHAPTER 29

EARLY MODERN INDIA AND IRAN

OUTLINE

OVERVIEW

The British conquest of India marked the first major territorial expansion of the West into Asia. Within a century, it had brought the major European powers to the Orient in search of markets, raw materials, and labor. The legacy of this would be the emergence of an Asian industrial giant, Japan; the world's largest socialist state, Communist China; and the world's largest democracy, India itself.

Britain's conquest was made possible by the virtual collapse of political authority in India in the first half of the eighteenth century. In this it served as a contrast to another ancient culture, that of Iran, which faced similar problems at the same time but was relatively more successful in dealing with them.

Both India and Iran faced the problem of dealing with rigid and corrupt dynasties in the early eighteenth century, and in both religious conflict was a complication as well. In Iran, the decadent Safavid dynasty, unable to cope with Ottoman pressure both against the throne and against the Shi'ite Muslim faith of most Iranians, was pushed aside by a native conqueror, Nadir Quli (Nadir Shah). Nadir attempted to bridge the conflict between Sunni and Shi'ite Muslims, but was rebuffed by both parties. At the same time, he pursued a policy of military adventurism; his invasion of India in 1739 revealed the hollowness of the Mughal dynasty and helped topple India into chaos. At last provoking rebellion in Iran, he was assassinated after a series of bloody purges. The peaceful administration of Karim Khan (who refused to claim the traditional title of shah) restored order and prosperity, however, and the Qajar dynasty that succeeded him, though increasingly subject to Western influence, was able to rule into the twentieth century.

The Mughal dynasty in India, like the Safavid in Iran, had grown more repressive but less capable. It ruled to all intents and purposes in name only after the reign of Aurangzeb (died 1707), but India's regional and cultural diversity made it difficult for an effective successor to emerge. Prolonged weakness invited the assaults of Nadir Shah and others, but no invader was able to do more than pillage the huge empire.

India's last conqueror was its most distant: Great Britain. Profit, not power, was the original motive for British interest in India, but a chartered trading venture, the English East India Company, was able to extend its control over the populous state of Bengal in the 1750s. From this base Britain proceeded slowly, until the threat of French interference during the European wars of 1793-1815 prompted it to extend its control over the remainder of the subcontinent, a process essentially completed by 1818. The feeble heirs of the Mughal dynasty continued to sit in Delhi, and about half the subcontinent and one-third of its population remained under native protectorates.

Although the British at first respected Indian customs, they gradually adopted a condescending and exploitative attitude. The advent of the Industrial Revolution opened India up as a market for British manufactures, ruining the native textile industry. Some

Britons continued to value and admire the achievements of Indian culture, and stimulated a scholarly renaissance among the Indians themselves. By the mid-nineteenth century however India had become the centerpiece of the British empire, and the crown tightened its hold on it, reducing the responsibility once jointly shared with the East India Company and working to eliminate native principalities. This brought it into conflict with Indian elites, and when mutiny broke out in the army in 1857 it quickly engulfed large areas of India in bloody rebellion. Most native units remained loyal to their British commanders however, and within a year the rebellion had been suppressed. Thenceforth, the British ruled as conquerors. They assassinated the last Mughal emperor and his heirs and eliminated the last vestiges of partnership with the East India Company, although they prudently avoided dispossessing more native princes. By 1858, the structure of British India as it was to endure until independence was essentially complete.

POINTS TO PONDER

1. Weak dynasties and religious division created anarchic conditions in both early eighteenth-century India and Iran.

2. Because of its great size and diversity, no native ruler was able to reestablish order in India.

3. The British conquest of India, though largely unplanned, was a fateful event not only for both parties but for Asia and the world.

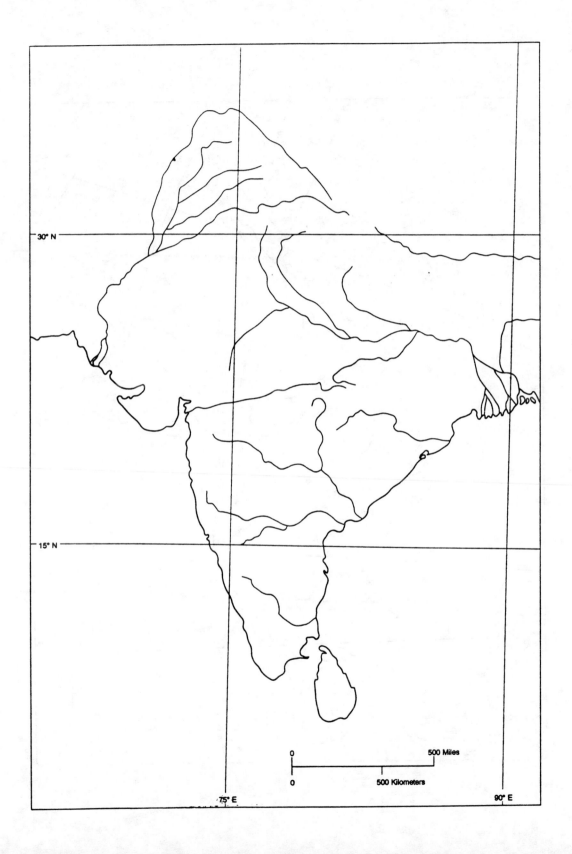

30° N

15° N

75° E

90° E

0   500 Miles

0   500 Kilometers

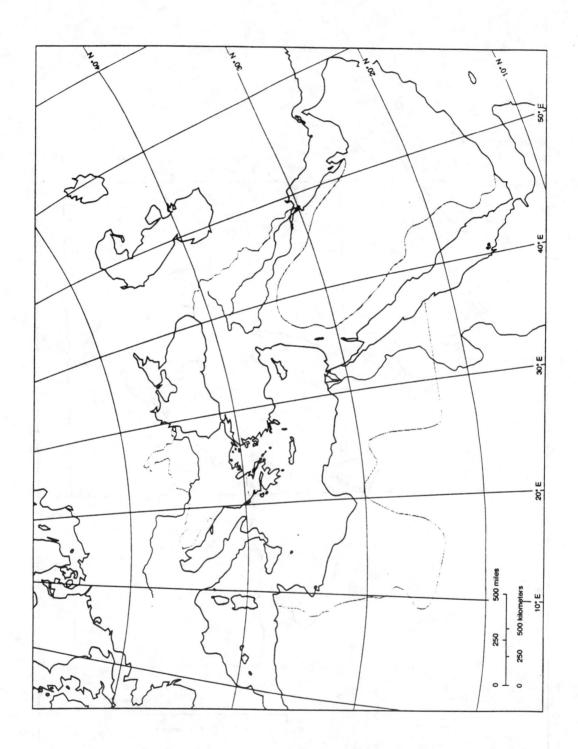

GEOGRAPHY

Locate the following on the first map:

Vindhya range	Kashmir
Deccan plateau	Punjab
Delhi	Hindu Kush
Gulf of Bengal	Ceylon (Kandy)
Madras	Trincomalee
Bombay	Colombo
Calcutta	Goa
Surat	Agra
Mysore	Simla
Hyderabad	Oudh
Maharashtra	Rajasthan

Locate the following on the second map:

Arabian Sea	Isfahan
Teheran	Shiraz
Gulf of Oman	Persian Gulf
Ottoman Empire	

1. How did Indian geography work both against political unification of the subcontinent and in favor of foreign invasion?

2. How was Nadir Shah's expansionist policy influenced in part by Iran's geographically exposed position?

CHRONOLOGY

Number the following in correct chronological sequence:

1. _____ Founding of Calcutta

2. _____ Nadir Shah seizes the throne of Iran

3. _____ Last armed Indian rebellion against British rule

4. _____ Vasco da Gama lands in Calicut

5. _____ Death of Karim Khan

6. _____ India Act

7. _____ British conquest of Ceylon

8. _____ Founding of the English (British) East India Company

9. _____ Battle of Plassey

IDENTIFICATION

1. Maratha Confederacy

2. Bengal

3. Joseph Dupleix

4. Nawab

5. Robert Clive

6. Black Hole of Calcutta

7. Mohun Roy

8. Sikhs

9. Sanskrit

10. Warren Hastings

11. Mutiny of 1857

12. Rabindranath Tagore

13. Safavid dynasty

14. Ja'fariyah sect

15. Agha Muhammad

DEFINITION

1. English East India Company

2. Orientalists

3. Bengal Renaissance

4. Zamindar

5. *Sati*

6. Sinhalese

7. Princely States

8. Qajar dynasty

COMPLETION

1. The earliest Western traders in modern Asia were the _____.

2. The first British base in India was established at _____.

3. The first major Indian territory conquered by the British was _____.

4. The connection between Indian and European languages was discovered by _____ _____.

5. The center of the Bengal Renaissance was the city of _____.

6. The British expedition destroyed by Afghan resisters was known as _____.

7. A new educational and penal code was devised for India by _____.

8. The last Mughal ruler of India was _____.

9. The greatest threat to Iranian security in the eighteenth century was posed by
_____.

10. The "Napoleon of Iran" was the nickname given to _____.

SHORT ANSWER

1. What products did European traders seek in Asia?

2. What caused the collapse of the Mughal dynasty?

3. Why were the British successful in defeating their imperial rivals in India?

4. How did partnership with the East India Company enable Britain to govern India with relatively little expenditure of money or personnel?

5. What were the basic principles of British educational reform in India?

6. How did British manufactures subordinate India's native industries?

7. Why did the British permit the Princely States to remain in India?

8. How were British attitudes toward India changed by the Mutiny of 1857?

9. How did the attitudes of native Indian elites toward the British differ from those of the ordinary population?

10. How was Karim Khan successful in restoring order to Iran?

UNDERSTANDING THE DOCUMENTS

1. How did the increase in taxation under the late Mughals indicate the decline of the dynasty?

2. What were some of the problems faced by European traders trying to gain a foothold on the Indian subcontinent in the late seventeenth century?

3. How does the testimony of Alexander Dow and William Jones show the disparity of early British attitudes toward India? What assumptions do both share about the value of Indian culture?

4. How does the behavior of the officials of the East India Company indicate the effects of their newly gained power and wealth?

TERM-PAPER TOPICS

Early European Traders in Asia
The East India Companies and Their Rivalries
The Decline of Mughal India
Robert Clive: Founder of Imperial India
The British Orientalists
Sati and the Status of Women in India
Calcutta: The Growth of a City
Changing British Attitudes Toward India
A World Apart: The Princely States and Their Rulers
Dwarkanath Tagore: Indian Entrepreneur
The British Reform of Indian Education
The Dual System in British India
The Mutiny of 1857
Nadir Quli: Napoleon of Iran
Religious Factions and Religious Minorities in Eighteenth-Century Iran

CHAPTER 30

MANCHU CHINA AND TOKUGAWA JAPAN

OUTLINE

OVERVIEW

Manchu China and Tokugawa Japan both represented successful consolidations of existing systems. The Manchus built on China's long imperial tradition, presiding over a period of unprecedented expansion, artistic brilliance, and general prosperity. The Tokugawa shogunate also represented a traditional solution to civil unrest, carried to the point of virtual isolation from the world but effective in its own terms.

The Manchus spoke a foreign tongue and, although largely assimilated to Chinese culture, were perceived as alien. They nonetheless won support by using Chinese as well as Manchu officials to govern the countryside, by rotating officials periodically to ensure against corruption, and by respecting the imperial tradition, particularly the examination system. The emperors Kang Hsi and Ch'ien Lung, who reigned 61 years apiece, set high standards, though these deteriorated in the later part of Ch'ien's reign. The burgeoning population was served by intensified agriculture and an enhanced communications network, including new roads and postal stations. Above all, since China's vast population, which approached 450 million by the mid-nineteenth century, was essentially self-regulating, the example of enlightened government from the throne assisted the local and familial controls by which order was maintained.

The Tokugawa shogunate, established by Tokugawa Ieyasu after a period of feudal warfare, gave Japan the most effective government it had ever known, although at a substantial price. The shoguns ruled the center of the country directly from Edo (Tokyo), and the remainder by vassals (*daimyos*) whose loyalty was pledged by hostages. Legitimacy rested with the emperor, who reigned but did not rule from his palace in Kyoto. The Tokugawa enforced their will through a system of close surveillance and hierarchical controls; all classes were subordinated to the feudal aristocracy, to whom they were required to make obeisance on pain of death. Foreigners were expelled, Christian converts were forced to recant or suffer death, and external trade ceased but for an annual visit by the Dutch. Even firearms were eliminated to maintain the dominance of the sword-wielding samurai elite. Nonetheless, the urban core of Japan prospered, and merchants gradually regained their status. While retaining an outward feudal rigidity, Japan remained a sophisticated society, and in the pleasure districts of the large cities, especially Edo, the classes mingled freely. Popular arts also flourished, including Kabuki theater and the woodblock prints of such masters as Hokusai and Hiroshige.

Both China and Japan faced dire challenges by the nineteenth century. In China, the Manchu (Ch'ing) dynasty had succumbed to corruption, while the soaring population had begun to outstrip the food supply. The pressures placed on it by Western powers were at first minor compared to these larger concerns, but would soon become serious. In Japan, the growth of a commercialized society created increasing tensions with its feudal framework. The arrival of Commodore Perry's squadron in 1853 forced the Tokugawa to readmit foreign traders, and precipitated a peaceful revolution, the Meiji Restoration, which would set Japan on the path to modernity.

POINTS TO PONDER

1. The Manchu dynasty was able to win loyalty by respecting traditional customs and relying upon established social controls.

2. The Tokugawa shogunate, also governing in a traditional manner, was flexible enough to permit commercial society to flourish.

3. Japan's urbanized society, although long isolated, was better able to respond to the challenges posed by Western commercial imperialism than China's peasant-based one.

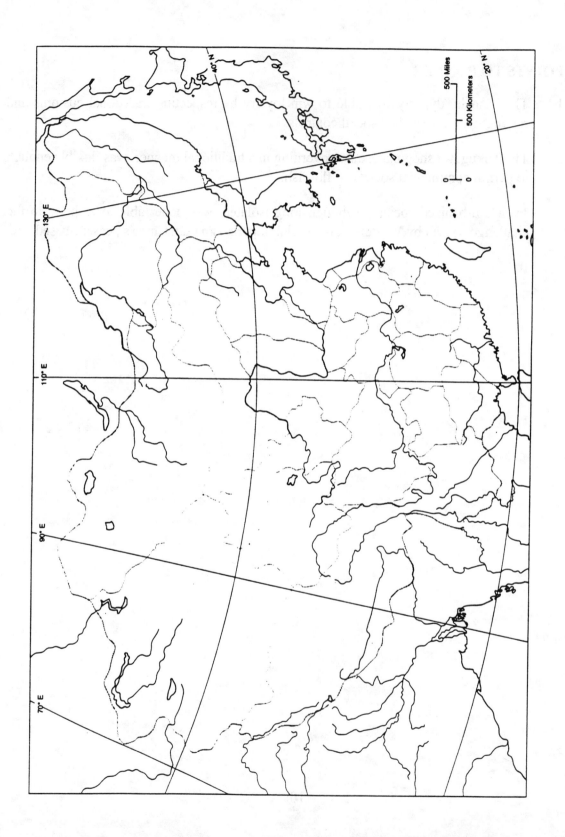

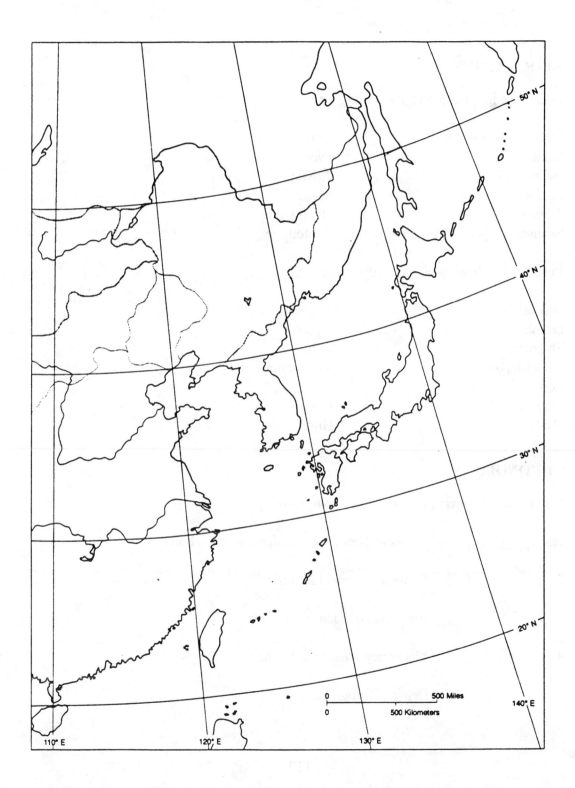

50° N

40° N

30° N

20° N

140° E

110° E   120° E   130° E

0   500 Miles

0   500 Kilometers

GEOGRAPHY

Locate the following on the first map:

Manchuria	Yenan
Korea	Szechuan
Great Wall	Taiwan
Peking	Macao
Tientsin	Hong Kong
Shanghai	Canton

Locate the following on the second map:

Hokkaido	Nagasaki
Honshu	Kyushu
Shikoku	Mito
Sea of Japan	Yokohama
Edo (Tokyo)	Kyoto
Nagoya	Kobe
Osaka	Hiroshima

CHRONOLOGY

Number the following in correct chronological sequence:

1. _____ Treaty of Nerchinsk confirms Russian border

2. _____ Portuguese arrival in Japan

3. _____ Accession of Manchu dynasty

4. _____ Macartney mission to China

5. _____ Death of Kang Hsi

6. _____ Beginning of Tokugawa shogunate

7. _____ Treaty of Nanking

8. _____ Uprising of the White Lotus sect

9. _____ Meiji Restoration

IDENTIFICATION

1. Manchu (Ch'ing) Dynasty

2. Kang Hsi

3. Ch'ien Lung

4. Ho–shen

5. Treaty of Nerchinsk

6. White Lotus sect

7. *Dream of the Red Chamber*

8.   Viscount Macartney

9.   Opium War

10.   Oda Nobunaga

11.   Toyotomi Hideyoshi

12.   Tokugawa Ieyasu

13.   Geisha

14.   *Noh*

15.   Haiku

DEFINITION

1. Examination system

2. Kowtow (k'e t'ou)

3. Unequal Treaties

4. Shogun

5. *Daimyo*

6. Shinto

7. "Floating World"

8. Meiji Restoration

COMPLETION

1.   The name of Ch'ing adopted by the Manchu dynasty meant _____.

2.   Chinese agriculture was enhanced by the importation of such crops as potatoes, corn, and peanuts from _____.

3.   China's borders were restored in Taiwan, Mongolia, and Tibet under the rule of _____.

4.   The chief problem facing China in the late eighteenth and nineteenth centuries was a sharp rise in _____.

5.   The only Chinese port where Westerners were permitted to trade in the eighteenth century was _____.

6.   Britain sought to penetrate the Chinese market through the sale of _____.

7.   The Ashikaga shogunate was destroyed by the unchecked power of the _____.

8.   Under the Tokugawa, the lowest social order was that of the _____ _____.

9.   A highly popular dramatic form introduced into Japan in the seventeenth century was _____.

10.   The Meiji Restoration was marked by a formal surrender of all feudal domains to _____.

SHORT ANSWER

1. How were the Manchu able to govern a population of 400 million with only about 30,000 officials?

2. Why did the image of Manchu China appeal to European thinkers of the Enlightenment?

3. How did the Chinese improve their agriculture to keep pace with their increasing population?

4. How did Kang Hsi attempt to promote education and learning?

5. How did the emphasis placed on family ties in China tend to foster corruption in government?

6. Why did the prosperity of China's commercial elites not lead to the development of entrepreneurial capitalism as in Europe?

7. How did the Tokugawa shoguns secure their power?

8. Why did the Tokugawa attempt to suppress Japan's thriving merchant elite?

9. How did the Floating World offer a relief from the rigidly hierarchical structure of Tokugawa society?

10. How did Japan's response to Western efforts to open up trade differ from that of China?

UNDERSTANDING THE DOCUMENTS

1. Why were European observers of the eighteenth century pessimistic about the chances for Western trade with China?

2. What does Hideyoshi's letter to his wife reveal about the status and duties of a lord's wife in feudal Japan?

3. How does the view of Japanese women given by American authors in the nineteenth century compare with Hideyoshi's expectation of his wife in the sixteenth? Whose position appears to be more genuinely respected?

TERM-PAPER TOPICS

The Arts of China and Japan
Chinese Contacts with the West before Macartney
Kang Hsi and the Expansion of Manchu China
Learning versus Creativity: The Imperial Examination System
Ch'ien Lung and His Court
Scientific Agriculture in Manchu China
Ho–shen and the Problem of Corruption in Manchu China
The Manchu System of Government
The Image of China in Eighteenth-Century Europe
Opium and Empire
Tokugawa Japan: The Last Feudal State
The Code of the Samurai
The "Floating World"
The Life and Art of Hokusai
The Perry Expedition and the Opening of Japan

CHAPTER 31

THE INDUSTRIAL REVOLUTION

OUTLINE

OVERVIEW

Until the nineteenth century, all labor involved a greater or lesser degree of human physical effort. Since then, work has been performed increasingly by machines powered by new energy sources. The enormous growth of productive capacity resulting from this has transformed work, society, and the face of the planet more than any event since the introduction of agriculture.

No single element determined Europe as the site of the Industrial Revolution. Other societies had faced subsistence crises that might have spurred technological innovation; others had had vigorous merchant elites ready to exploit new products and techniques. Instead we must look to a combination of factors, none decisive in itself but all complementary. Europe's mechanical arts had developed considerably since the sixteenth century, particularly in mining and metallurgy. The Scientific Revolution, with its emphasis on experimentation, had proved fruitful for invention. Exploration, conquest, and the beginning of a global economy had furnished distant markets, stretched naval capacity, and developed innovative entrepreneurial and credit schemes. Population had begun to rise sharply in the eighteenth century, straining traditional resources and existing productive strength.

Britain was well-placed at this juncture of forces. It had replaced the Netherlands as the world's leading naval power in the seventeenth century, and would replace it as the center of European finance in the eighteenth. It had a stable government, a thoroughly commercialized agriculture, and abundant coal and iron, the key natural resources of the Industrial Revolution. It also had a target industry for development, textiles, and, after the conquest of Bengal, a huge captive market. It was resilient enough socially to sustain an Industrial Revolution without succumbing to a political one. Nonetheless, it experienced great strain, and its new industrial laboring class, largely recruited by systematic rural depopulation, great suffering. The exploitation of female and child labor had a devastating effect on the health and welfare of much of the population. The first quarter of the nineteenth century produced radical demands for reform such as those of Robert Owen, and by the second quarter, even conservatives were ready to support factory legislation. Yet by mid-century industrialization had made Britain the richest and most powerful state in the world.

Industrialization had spread to the Continent by 1830, with much of western Europe repeating Britain's social experience in the next two generations, although without its success in containing political upheaval. After 1850, applied science was increasingly called to the aid of technology, while basic advances in chemistry and electromagnetism greatly extended its scope. Rapid population growth and urbanization followed, with industrial Manchester serving as the prototype of many cities on the Continent. By the end of the century, a majority of the population was housed in these cities, and agriculture had become a minority occupation. By that time as well, industrial capitalism had penetrated to the farthest corners of the globe, transforming human society with a force unparalleled in history.

POINTS TO PONDER

1. The Industrial Revolution was the product of many forces, economic, political, demographic, and technological, no single one of which was dominant.

2. In pioneering the Industrial Revolution, Britain enjoyed the particular advantages of stable government, flexible capital, and a navy capable of securing distant markets.

3. The spread of industrialization transformed human society more profoundly than any development since the invention of agriculture.

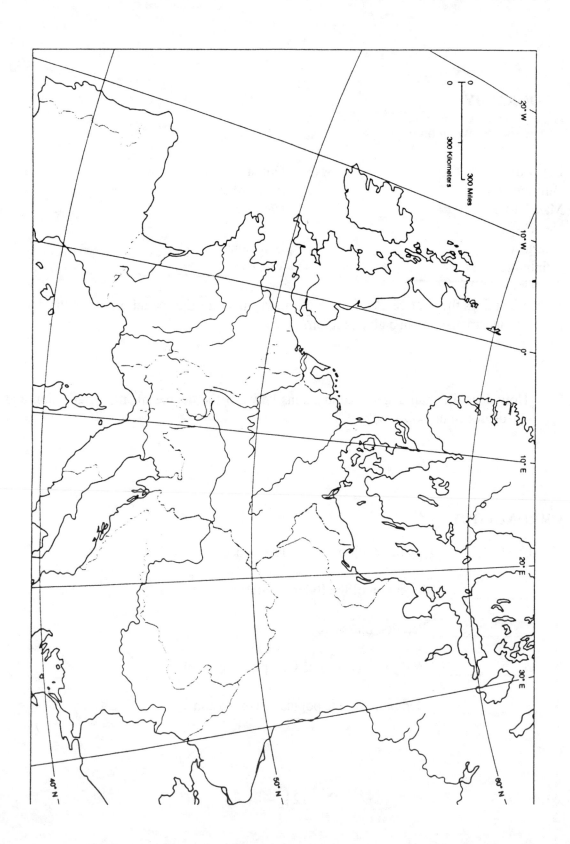

GEOGRAPHY

Locate the following on the map:

London	Dublin
Birmingham	Amsterdam
Manchester	Hamburg
Newcastle	Milan
Glasgow	Barcelona
Edinburgh	Vienna

1. What does the relative distribution of railway track in Europe tell us about the degree of industrialization in a given region?

2. How does the map suggest connections between the degree of industrialization and the degree of urbanization?

CHRONOLOGY

Number the following in correct chronological sequence:

1. _____ Invention of the flying shuttle

2. _____ Peterloo massacre

3. _____ *Zollverein* (Customs Union) in Germany

4. _____ Beginning of the population explosion

124

5. _____ Ten-hour working day enacted in Britain

6. _____ Development of the combustion engine

7. _____ Darby's coke-smelting process for iron

8. _____ Anti-Combination acts

9. _____ Owen's model industrial colony at New Lanark

IDENTIFICATION

1. Windmill

2. Spinning jenny

3. Coke

4. James Watt

5. Thomas Malthus

6. Richard Arkwright

7.   Factory

8.   Poor Law (1834)

9.   Adam Smith

10.   David Ricardo

11.   Karl Marx

12.   Luddism

13.   Grand Union

14.   *Zollverein*

15.   Crystal Palace

DEFINITION

1. Industrial Revolution

2. Agricultural Revolution

3. Capitalism

4. Cottage (domestic) system

5. *Laissez-faire*

6. Physiocrats

7. Smelting

8. Population explosion

COMPLETION

1. The principal source of energy in preindustrial Europe was _____.

2. The puddling process converted _____ into _____.

3. Karl Marx and Friedrich Engels identified the _____ as the most important social element in the Industrial Revolution.

4. Workdays of up to _____ were not uncommon in the early days of the Industrial Revolution.

5. Thomas Malthus warned of the dangers of unchecked demographic expansion in his _____.

6. The Scots philanthropist who set up the first cooperative communities was _____ _____.

7. The most important single reason for the dramatic decrease in Western mortality rates after 1850 was improved _____.

8. The largest city in the world in the nineteenth century was _____.

9. The most important means of conveying goods during the nineteenth century was the _____.

10. The largest industrial power in the world in 1900 was _____.

SHORT ANSWER

1. How does commercial capitalism differ from industrial capitalism?

2. What is the distinction between subsistence and commercial agriculture?

3. How was agricultural productivity improved in eighteenth-century Britain?

4. How did enclosure contribute to the formation of an industrial proletariat in Britain?

5. How did the end of seigneurial feudalism retard the development of industrialization in France?

6. How was family life among the proletariat affected by the industrial system of early nineteenth-century Britain?

7. Why did many workers attempt to prevent the introduction of new machines into their trades?

8. Why did Robert Owen think that industrial capitalism was opposed to genuine social progress?

9. Why did the Industrial Revolution lead to the growth of cities?

10. How did scientific advances promote the expansion of industry after 1850?

UNDERSTANDING THE DOCUMENTS

1. What according to Malthus are the major checks operating on the increase of human population?

2. What does the testimony of Joseph Hebergam indicate about employer attitudes toward labor in the early Industrial Revolution?

3. What are the objections to mechanized production raised by "Ned Ludd"? How do they indicate the values of traditional artisans?

4. How do the two views of Manchester reflect its transformation from a commercial to an industrial center?

TERM-PAPER TOPICS

Agriculture and the Industrial Revolution
The Dutch as Precursors of the Industrial Revolution
The Age of Steam
The Factory System
Life in a Factory Town
The Impact of the Railway
Thomas Robert Malthus and the Population Question
Industrial Utopias: Owen, Fourier, and the Cooperative Movement
Adam Smith: Defender of Capitalism
Marx's Interpretation of the Industrial Revolution
Ill Fares the Land: The Social Consequences of Enclosure
The Poor Laws and the Management of Labor
Gold and the Industrial Revolution
Science and the Industrial Revolution
Thomas Alva Edison, Inventor

CHAPTER 32

THE AGE OF IDEOLOGY

OUTLINE

OVERVIEW

The defeat of Napoleon and the restoration of the Bourbon dynasty in France signaled not the end but the beginning of an age of rapid social change, class polarization, and political struggle. The contending groups—noble and bourgeois, bourgeois and proletarian—expressed their opposition by means of ideologies which embodied not only the vision and aspiration of each group but which claimed universal validity. *Liberalism* was the specific ideology of the bourgeoisie and *socialism* emerged as that of the working class or at any rate its supporters, while the appeal of *nationalism* cut across both groups. At the same time, the Romantic movement in the arts, which partook of all these ideologies in its search for meaning, reflected the striving and turmoil of the age.

The pressure of liberalism and nationalism on established regimes was the major political theme of the period. The powers that assembled at Vienna in 1815 were represented by traditional elites that attempted, as far as possible, to restore the world as it had existed before 1789. This attempt was doomed to failure, both because of the conflicting interests of the powers themselves and the strength of the forces for change within each of them. Only Britain would be able to avert revolution in the generation ahead. Broadly speaking, the bourgeoisie led the revolutions that broke out in 1830, and fought the proletariat for control of those that erupted in 1848. Elite consolidation resulted in patterns of accommodation between the bourgeoisie and the nobility. Such accommodation was most successful in Britain, where a long period of elite unity, the Victorian consensus, emerged, and least so in France, where class conflict remained overt. Unfulfilled national aspirations would continue to dominate the politics of Germany and Italy before and after 1848.

The Romantic movement that began in the eighteenth century and came to full flower in the nineteenth replaced traditional authority with an ethos of individual creativity. Many Romantic artists were involved directly in the political struggles of the period. The Romantic achievement itself, particularly in music and poetry, remains the basic context of Western culture to this day. It is significant too as the first artistic movement in which women played a central role.

POINTS TO PONDER

1.   The social classes that emerged in the early nineteenth century each tended to define itself in terms of a specific ideology.

2.   The powerful force of nationalism was the one sentiment that cut across ideological lines among all classes.

3.   Romanticism reflected the search for individual meaning in an age of conflict.

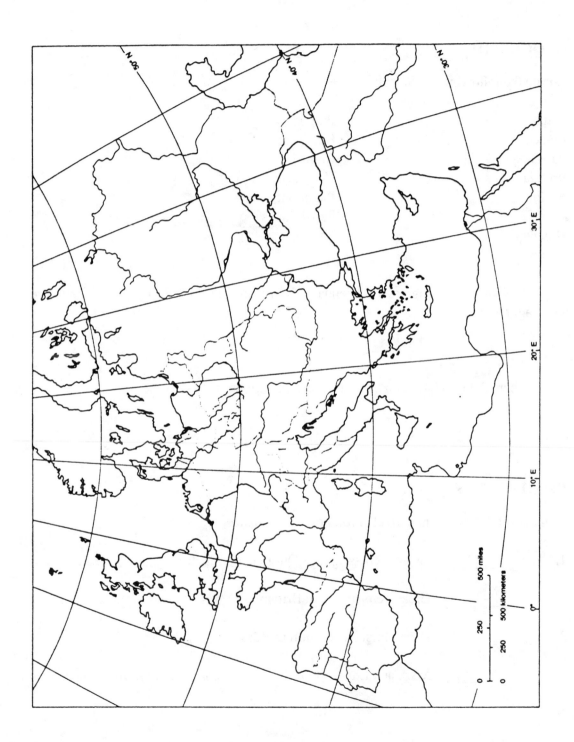

GEOGRAPHY

Locate the following on the map:

Britain	Prague
France	Budapest
Paris	Rome
Prussia	Venetia
Berlin	Piedmont
Austria	Papal States
Hungary	Naples
Vienna	

1.   How did the Congress of Vienna redesign the map of Europe to contain French aggression?

2.   Where did revolution threaten the Austrian empire in 1848?

CHRONOLOGY

Number the following in correct chronological sequence:

1.   _____ Greece rebels against Ottoman domination

2.   _____ Great Reform Bill in Britain

3.   _____ Decembrist Revolution in Russia

4.   _____ Marx and Engels publish *The Communist Manifesto*

5. _____ Quadruple Alliance

6. _____ Orléans dynasty comes to power in France

7. _____ Goethe's *The Sorrows of Young Werther* pioneers the Romantic

   movement in Germany

8. _____ Flight of Metternich from Vienna

9. _____ People's Charter in Britain

IDENTIFICATION

1. Congress of Vienna

2. Prince Metternich

3. Quadruple Alliance

4. Six Acts

5. Ultras

6. Nicholas I

7.   July Revolution

8.   Louis-Philippe

9.   Chartists

10. Goethe

11. *Capital*

12. Frankfurt Assembly

13. Madame de Staël

14. Giuseppe Mazzini

15. June Days

DEFINITION

1. Ideology

2. Congress System

3. Romanticism

4. Nationalism

5. Utopian Socialists

6. Rotten boroughs

7. Iron Law of Wages

8. Dictatorship of the proletariat

COMPLETION

1. The largest territorial gainer at the Congress of Vienna was _____.

2. The doctrine that the great powers could intervene in the affairs of any state to prevent

   revolution was enunciated in the _____.

3. The Decembrist revolt attempted to bring constitutional government to

   _____.

4. The Romantic movement in English poetry began with the work of

   _____ and _____.

5. The role of great personalities in history was emphasized by the German philosopher

   _____.

6. A famous symbolic painting of the July Revolution was _____

   _____ by _____.

7. Control of society by a technocratic elite of scientists and engineers was advocated by

   _____.

8. The leading socialist thinker of the nineteenth century was _____.

9. The Hungarian revolution of 1848 was led by _____.

10. The movement for Italian unification was led by the state of _____.

SHORT ANSWER

1. What were the aims of Metternich at the Congress of Vienna?

2. What is meant by the "Concert of Europe?"

3. What was the impact of the Greek revolution on European politics?

4. Why did Romanticism concentrate on the heroic individual?

5. Why did the restored Bourbon monarchy in France collapse after only fifteen years?

6. What did the Reform Bill of 1832 in Britain accomplish? What did it leave undone?

7. What were the demands of the Chartists?

8. What did Karl Marx mean by the idea of the class struggle?

9. How was nationalism a driving force in the revolutions of 1830 and 1848?

10. Why did the Frankfurt Assembly fail to unite Germany in 1848?

UNDERSTANDING THE DOCUMENTS

1. How does De Maistre use the idea of a "national mind" to combat what he regards as the harmful effects of individualism?

2. How does Metternich's view of revolution suggest that it can only be the work of malcontents, and never the will of the people?

3. How does Wordsworth's image of the poet suggest a view of the artist as a defender of universal values? Do you think De Maistre or Metternich would have agreed with this view? Why?

4. How does Mazzini invoke the same ideas as De Maistre—God and community—to reach entirely different conclusions about the legitimacy of revolution and the proper form of government? How does he suggest that education and insurrection mutually support each other in the work of revolution?

5. How does De Tocqueville's account of the June Days of 1848 support Marx's theory of the class struggle?

TERM-PAPER TOPICS

The Congress of Vienna
The Bourbon Restoration in France
The Greek Struggle for Independence
Russia: Revolution and Reaction
Goethe and the Romantic Spirit
Delacroix: Artist of Revolution
Romanticism and the Cult of Genius
Women and the Romantic Novel
The Struggle for Gender Equality in the Romantic Era
The July Monarchy
The Making of the Reform Bill in Britain
The Chartists
The Classical Liberals
The Socialist Challenge
The Revolutions of 1848

CHAPTER 33

THE TRIUMPH OF NATIONALISM

OUTLINE

OVERVIEW

Italian and German nationalists were bitterly disappointed at the failure of the revolutions of 1848. Those revolutions revealed the difficulty of trying to build a nation without a firm territorial base and an army committed to the task of unification. These problems were solved in Italy by Piedmont under the leadership of Count Camilio di Cavour, and in Germany by Prussia under Otto von Bismarck. Both men faced formidable obstacles, and neither began with a clear vision of unification; Bismarck had actually opposed the revolutionaries of 1848. Both were led beyond their initial intentions by circumstances. Cavour, having used French forces to unite most of northern Italy under Piedmont's rule, was obliged to annex the remainder of the peninsula when Giuseppe Garibaldi attacked the Kingdom of the Two Sicilies. Bismarck likewise found himself forced to complete the unification of Germany to avert the loss of the Catholic south to Austria.

While unification was proceeding in Italy and Germany, bourgeois elites were consolidating their power in Britain and France, and the industrial North imposed its will on the planter aristocracy of the South in the American Civil War. At the same time, the major powers of eastern Europe, Austria and Russia, were attempting to adapt both government and society to the changing circumstances of the nineteenth-century world. Nationalism also inspired the Jews of Europe to seek a homeland of their own.

In Britain, a new ruling elite emerged dedicated to expansion through overseas empire. Napoleon III sought to suppress the class conflict that had erupted openly in France in 1848 and to unite the country on the basis of authoritarian controls, commercial prosperity, and imperial posturing. He enjoyed some success until domestic unrest and military defeat unseated him, establishing a pattern that twentieth-century dictators would emulate. Americans were tested far more grievously in a bloody civil war until the Union prevailed over the secessionist South, whose defeat removed slavery and opened the way to a rapid growth based on free labor and mass immigration. By the end of the century, the United States had become the world's leading industrial power.

Deeply divided by the nationalist aspirations of its ethnic minorities, Austria would attempt to stabilize itself in the wake of defeats in Italy and Germany that removed its traditional presence in both areas. The peace it made with Hungary in 1867 granted virtual autonomy to the latter and established the Dual Monarchy. In Russia, the emancipation of the serfs by Tsar Alexander II was the key to a reform program aimed at modernizing the country after its defeat in the Crimean War. The reforms satisfied neither the peasantry nor the intelligentsia, however, and with Alexander's assassination in 1881 Russia plunged again into reaction. Turkey, the proverbial "Sick Man of Europe," survived only at the sufferance of the great powers; an attempt at reform was aborted by Abdul Hamid II, and a modernizing revolution was postponed until the twentieth century.

Isolated by the rising nationalist fervor throughout Europe, the Jews sought identity and security in a nation of their own. Although many migrated to the Western hemisphere, Theodor Herzl's Zionist movement revived ancestral hopes of a return to Palestine, a dream realized only in the wake of the Holocaust.

POINTS TO PONDER

1. The nationalist revolutions of 1848 in Italy and Germany were completed not by revolutionaries but by the leaders of established states, Piedmont and Prussia.

2. Nationalism was exploited by Napoleon III as a means of suppressing class conflict in France.

3. The abolition of slavery in the United States and of serfdom in Russia were both keys to industrial modernization, although Russia's reforms failed to displace a reactionary elite while the planter aristocracy of the American South was eliminated by the Civil War.

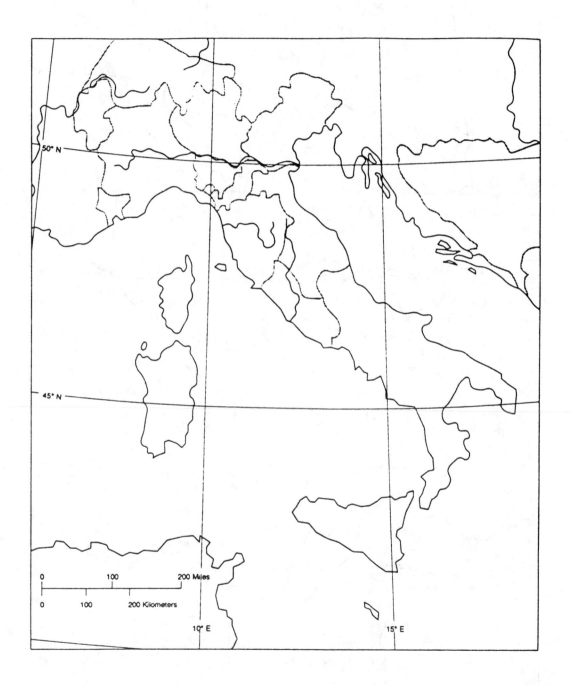

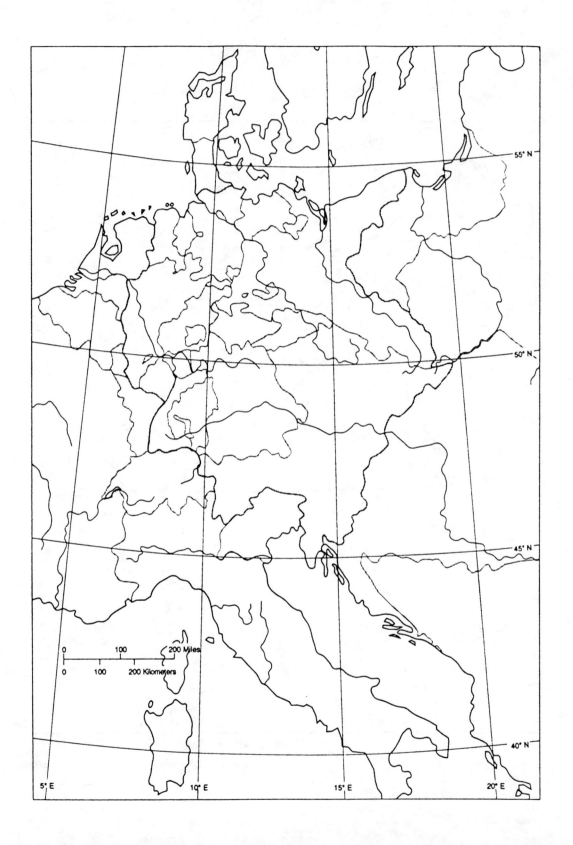

55° N

50° N

45° N

40° N

0   100   200 Miles

0   100   200 Kilometers

5° E   10° E   15° E   20° E

GEOGRAPHY

Locate the following on the first map:

Piedmont
Savoy
Lombardy
Venetia
Tuscany
The Romagna

Sicily
Kingdom of the Two Sicilies
Naples
Rome
The Papal States

Locate the following on the second map:

Prussia
Schleswig
Holstein
Hanover
Bavaria
Sedan
Vienna
Bohemia

Alsace
Lorraine
Serbia
Saxony
Württemberg
Austria
Hungary

1. How did Bismarck exploit Prussia's commanding geographical position to achieve the unification of Germany?

2. Why did Garibaldi's invasion of the Kingdom of the Two Sicilies force Cavour's hand in completing the unification of Italy?

CHRONOLOGY

Number the following in correct chronological sequence:

1. _____ Alexander II emancipates the serfs

2. _____ First Zionist Congress in Basel

3. _____ Louis-Napoleon assumes dictatorial power in France

4. _____ Treaty of Plombières

5. _____ Battle of Sedan

6. _____ Establishment of the Dual Monarchy

7. _____ Schleswig-Holstein dispute

8. _____ Garibaldi invades Sicily

9. _____ Crimean War

IDENTIFICATION

1. Crédit Mobilier

2. Baron Haussmann

3. Liberal Empire

4.   Maria Deraismes

5.   Giuseppe Mazzini

6.   Benito Juarez

7.   Red Shirts

8.   Junker

9.   German Confederation

10.   Hohenzollern dynasty

11.   *Ausgleich*

12.   Karl Lüger

13. Alexander Herzen

14. *Mir*

15. Theodor Herzl

DEFINITION

1. Second Empire

2. *Risorgimento*

3. Papal States

4. Dual Monarchy

5. Vienna Secession

6. Slavophiles

7. "Propaganda of the deed"

8. Eastern Question

COMPLETION

1. The emergence of _____ in Europe in the last half of the nineteenth century was a phenomenon of immense importance for the development of twentieth-century states around the world.

2. The regime that succeeded the Orléans dynasty in France was _____.

3. To demonstrate his popular support, Napoleon III made use of public referendums known as _____.

4. The unification of Italy was strenuously opposed by Pope _____.

5. William I of Prussia sought to break the deadlock over his controversial military reform bill by appointing _____ as minister-president.

6. The name given by Bismarck for his general political approach was _____.

7. The immediate cause of the outbreak of the Franco-Prussian War was the

   _____.

8. The dominant population group in Hungary was _____.

9. The _____ were Russian intellectuals who sought to

   achieve political goals.

10. Systematic attacks against Jewish lives and property in Russia often instigated by the

    authorities, were known as _____.

SHORT ANSWER

1. How was Louis–Napoleon, a virtual unknown, able to win election as President of
   France in 1848?

2. What were Napoleon III's reasons for sponsoring the massive reconstruction of Paris
   in the 1850s?

3. How did Cavour exploit Napoleon III in bringing about the unification of Italy?

4. What problems remained for Italy to face after unification?

5. Why did Austria attempt to block the unification of Germany by Prussia?

6. Why did the Treaty of Frankfurt confirm the end of the Concert of Europe?

7. What problems remained to face the Austrian empire after the establishment of the Dual Monarchy?

8. Why did the reforms of Alexander II fail to satisfy the peasantry and intelligentsia in Russia?

9. How did the decline of the Ottoman Empire affect the balance of power in eastern Europe?

10. Why did the Zionists regard the establishment of a homeland in Palestine as the only solution to the Jewish problem?

UNDERSTANDING THE DOCUMENTS

1. How did Louis–Napoleon connect Napoleon with the idea of liberty?

2. Why did Cavour see Garibaldi's invasion of Sicily as a grave threat to the interests of Piedmont?

3. How does the open letter from the "Will of the People" to Alexander III reflect the absence of moderate alternatives in tsarist Russia?

4. How do Herzl and Nordau interpret the phenomenon of anti-Semitism? What reasons do they suggest for its existence?

TERM-PAPER TOPICS

The Life and Death of the Second Republic
Napoleon III: Statesman or Dictator?
The Reconstruction of Paris
Napoleon III's Mexican Adventure
French Feminism and the Liberal Empire
The Roots of the *Risorgimento*
Cavour and Garibaldi: The Unlikely Alliance
Cavour and Bismarck: Two Roads to Unification
Bismarck and the Liberals
The Ems Dispatch
Vienna: Imperial Capital
The Fate of the Balkans
Russia's Radical Youth
The Odyssey of Theodor Herzl
The Crisis of the American Republic

CHAPTER 34

INDUSTRIAL SOCIETY AND THE LIBERAL ORDER

OUTLINE

OVERVIEW

The generation after 1871 saw the consolidation of industrial capitalism and the regime of liberalism. It was an age of unprecedented material prosperity but also of persistent and widening inequality between rich and poor, only modestly alleviated by the beginnings of the welfare state. While Social Darwinism extolled acquisitiveness and domination as virtues inherent in nature, representatives of the social and demographic majorities—workers and women—proposed their own demands to the dominant value system, and put forward, under the banners of socialism and feminism, their own conceptions of social justice.

The late nineteenth century also saw the rise of monopoly capitalism, popularly known as big business. The prevalence of monopoly in such major industries as steel, rail, and finance had significant effects on the class and occupational structure of the West. Wealth increased, but was concentrated in fewer and fewer hands; an unpropertied white collar middle class grew, largely out of the working class, but faced chronic insecurity; gains in production outpaced gains in wages; and farm incomes were depressed, stimulating migration to the cities and emigration abroad. The parliamentary regimes which had become characteristic of the West, though based on restricted suffrage (almost nowhere extended to women before World War I), became the focus of political struggle, and for some the targets of revolution.

Movements for social change were sharply divided in this period. Some feminists sought to gain legal equality and sexual emancipation for women as goals in themselves, while others felt they could be meaningful only within a transformed social order. Socialists differed too, with some continuing to espouse violent revolution and others hoping for peaceful change. The wider culture was also in flux. Traditional assumptions were challenged by Darwinism, which reinforced material optimism, most commonly expressed by the doctrine of progress, yet fostered spiritual pessimism among those who found the divine origin of humankind incompatible with the theory of evolution. Critics such as Spencer and Bagehot found in Darwinism a justification for existing social arrangements, while artists such as Dickens and Zola exposed the underside of industrial life, and Flaubert, Ibsen, and Tolstoy depicted the plight of women. More successful than ever before in the extent of its wealth and the range of its power, the West was thus profoundly divided as well.

POINTS TO PONDER

1. Big business became the characteristic form of industrial organization in the last decades of the nineteenth century.

2. The emergence of a white collar class, the decline of farm income and population, and mass emigration were some of the consequences of industrial change.

3. Socialists and feminists were divided in this period between those who hoped to change society by peaceful reform and those who remained committed to revolution.

CHRONOLOGY

Number the following in correct chronological sequence:

1. _____ Extension of the vote to middle–class males in Britain

2. _____ Formation of the Social Democratic Party in Germany

3. _____ Pankhurst founds the Women's Social and Political Union (WSPU)

4. _____ Publication of Darwin's *On the Origin of Species*

5. _____ Bernstein's *Evolutionary Socialism* challenges the Marxist doctrine

    of revolution

6. _____ Death of Queen Victoria

7. _____ Suppression of the Paris Commune

8. _____ Dreyfus pardoned

9. _____ Ibsen's *A Doll's House*

IDENTIFICATION

1. Henry Ford

2. Paris Commune

3. Long Depression

4. Bon Marché

5. Oscar Wilde

6. William Gladstone

7. Declaration of Sentiments

8. John Stuart Mill

9. Emily Davison

10. Auguste Comte

11. Herbert Spencer

12. Third Republic

13. Claude Monet

14. John Pierpont Morgan

15. Clara Zetkin

DEFINITION

1. Second Industrial Revolution

2. Limited liability

3. Vertical integration

4. Cult of domesticity

5. Liberalism

6. Suffragettes

7. Cartels

8. Impressionism

COMPLETION

1. The grandmother of both William II of Germany and Nicholas II of Russia was

   _____.

2. The two major political parties in nineteenth-century Britain were the

   _____ and the _____.

3. The conviction of Captain Dreyfus was publicly challenged by the novelist

   _____ _____.

4. Bismarck called his struggle against the influence of the papacy the _____.

5. _____ was the system of forming coalition governments on the basis

   of patronage rather than formal political parties.

6. The Spanish intellectuals who attempted to renovate Spain in the wake of its defeat by

   the United States were known as _____.

7. The application of ideas drawn from evolutionary biology to the problems of human

   society was known as _____.

8. Marx clashed with _____ for control of the First International.

9. Rosa Luxemburg and Georges Sorel advocated _____ as a

   tactic of revolutionary action.

10. _____ and _____

    challenged the British prohibition on disseminating information on birth control.

SHORT ANSWER

1. Why did the bourgeoisie and the aristocracy tend to merge into a single elite during the later nineteenth century?

2. Why did so few women remain in the work force after marriage in the nineteenth century?

3. What was meant by the "double standard" of sexual morality?

4. How did the Paris Commune contribute to the polarization of French politics and society?

5. Why did Bismarck initiate welfare state programs in Germany during the 1880s?

6. How did the "Roman question" undermine the legitimacy of the new Italian state?

7. What were the major goals sought by feminist reformers in the nineteenth century?

8. Why was Darwin's theory of evolution a challenge to accepted religious beliefs?

9. What were the artistic and political goals of the literary realists?

10. How did the anarchists differ in their approach to revolution from other socialists?

UNDERSTANDING THE DOCUMENTS

1. What are the chief responsibilities of bourgeois household management according to Mrs. Beeton's handbook? What social values is it intended to uphold?

2. Which tactics does Emmeline Pankhurst suggest for British suffragists to adopt in their struggle, and which to avoid?

3. Why did Kropotkin stress the importance of particular actions in fostering the spirit of revolt?

4. How does Angelica Balabanoff differ from Emmeline Pankhurst in her approach to the problems of feminine emancipation?

TERM-PAPER TOPICS

The Growth of Monopoly Capitalism
Science and the Doctrine of Progress
The Second Industrial Revolution
The Cult of Domesticity in the Nineteenth Century
Victoria, Symbol of an Age
The Paris Commune
The Dreyfus Affair
The Politics of Sexual Liberation
Emmeline Pankhurst: Pioneer Feminist
Before Darwin: The Evolution of Evolution
Social Darwinism: Theory and Ideology
The Impressionists and Their World
The Literary Realists
The Growth of Trade Unions
The Suffrage Movement

GLOBAL ESSAY

WRITING AND COMMUNICATION (II)

OVERVIEW

Writing was the principal means of communication over a distance from the first civilizations down to the nineteenth century. Literacy was for most of this period the privilege of the few, in part because of the difficulty and expense of book production, and in part because the ability to keep records, preserve laws, and interpret sacred texts were functions reserved by the elite. The Chinese were the first to invent both paper and movable type, but literacy spread only slowly from the elite to the merchant classes.

In contrast, the introduction of movable type to the less stratified societies of Europe in the fifteenth century had immediate and far-reaching consequences. Literature of every kind, from bibles to horoscopes, reached a wide public, and both Catholics and Protestants used print in the controversies of the Reformation. Newspapers had emerged by the seventeenth century, and the Enlightenment, which gave unprecedented power and prestige to a new class of secular intellectuals, the *philosophes*, was a phenomenon of print. The rise of science, too, was no less dependent on the dissemination of information and new knowledge that only print could make speedily available. As in China, a host of new literary forms developed, including various forms of fiction and popular manuals of every kind.

The nineteenth century saw the majority of the population in western Europe become literate, but it witnessed too the birth of new forms of communication and transmission, notably cable, telegraph, telephone, and film. These made communication at a distance possible even for the uneducated, while the spread of Western colonialism brought literacy to millions around the globe, and systems of writing to nonliterate societies. The communications revolution continued and expanded in the twentieth century with the development of radio, motion pictures, the phonograph, television, computers, and communications satellites. These inventions have facilitated both democracy and dictatorship, creating the mass societies of today with their susceptibility to propaganda but also world opinion with its power to affect events in every corner of the globe. Indeed, the power to communicate is fast outrunning the power to control the flow of information or even comprehend it. Despite this, the written word still retains its unique power to move, provoke, delight, and inform.

IDENTIFICATION

1. Parchment

2. Movable type

3. Gutenberg Bible

4. George Thomason

5. Julius Reuter

6. Mathew Brady

7. Guglielmo Marconi

8. Communications satellites

COMPLETION

1. The first printed book was published in China in the _____ century.

2. Papermaking spread to Europe through _____ traders.

3. The spread of literacy and printed books in sixteenth-century Europe was stimulated by the controversies of the _____.

4. Pamphleteering was critically important to the spread of ideas and information in the English, American, and French _____.

5. A captured French telegram, the _____, was a crucial factor in the outbreak of the Franco-Prussian War.

6. Immediate pictorial images could be transmitted for the first time with the development of _____.

7. The culture of _____ was largely an oral one before the nineteenth century.

8. The first major conflict in which television played a major role in shaping public response was _____.

SHORT ANSWER

1. Why did the invention of paper and printing in China not lead to mass literacy?

2. How did print lead to the formation of a new and more independent public opinion in the West?

3. How did print affect the transmission of the Scientific Revolution?

4. What new forms of communication facilitated the spread of books and newspapers in the nineteenth century?

5. What common literary forms developed both in China and the West?

6. What was the role of Western missionaries in spreading literacy around the globe?

7. What dangers do computer-programmed responses pose to the capacity for human decision-making in time of crisis?

TERM-PAPER TOPICS

Bookmaking in the Ancient World
The Book as Art: Illuminated Manuscripts and Chinese Calligraphy
The Battle of the Books: The Reformation in Print
Pamphleteers of Revolution: Tom Paine and the Abbé Sieyès
The Growth of Literacy in Preindustrial Europe
The Age of the Novel
Still and Moving Images: The Impact of the Camera on Modern Culture
The Computer Revolution

CHAPTER 35

THE AGE OF WESTERN DOMINATION

OUTLINE

OVERVIEW

During the last three decades of the nineteenth century, the Western powers expanded their empires to include direct control over almost all of Africa, and directly or indirectly over virtually the whole of Asia and the Pacific. By the beginning of the twentieth century, some four-fifths of the world was subject to Western domination, and to the transforming influence of industrial capitalism. The result was the establishment of complex forms of interdependency among the world's civilizations, and the beginnings of an international culture.

Liberal and Marxist scholars offered explanations for imperialism based on the defects of capitalism itself; later critics emphasized the role of elites both in the metropolis and the colonial periphery. Proponents of imperialism stressed the duty of the West to impose its material and moral standards on the rest of the world. Western imperialism was in fact a complex phenomenon in which economic, political, and sometimes altruistic motives were inextricably entwined. The drive for markets, exploitable labor, and natural resources was clearly present in most cases, yet colonies and even whole empires were acquired that were unproductive and economically draining, as in the case of Italy. Political prestige was an increasingly significant factor in colonization, but colonies were also sometimes acquired simply to fend off competitors, or in response to the initiative of traders, missionaries, and adventurers.

The forms of imperialism varied with the circumstances and opportunities of each region. In North Africa, settled governments made it possible to establish protectorates, whereas in much of sub-Saharan Africa the absence of centralized authority resulted in more direct control, including semiprivate ventures such as the Congo Free State and Rhodesia. British India evolved from a condominium to direct imperial status, although hundreds of nominal princely states remained. Southeast Asia was ruled in part directly, in part through native sultanates, though its active middlemen were Chinese migrants.

China itself, too large to be assimilated, was economically divided among the major industrial powers. These included Japan, which by adopting Western technology and methods became one of the few non-Western states to retain its independence and even to expand its territory during this period. Japan's defeat of both China and Russia established it as a world power, and shattered the myth of Western invincibility.

The impact of Western imperialism on the world's peoples was profound and continuing. Traditional values and institutions were challenged and overthrown, and traditional authority weakened or eclipsed. Declining death rates led to sometimes unchecked population growth; elites prospered, but general living standards fell. In the Congo, Australia, and New Zealand, native populations were decimated. Western values were sometimes embraced, sometimes resisted, and sometimes adapted to traditional norms. What they imposed, for good or ill, was a single common standard upon the varied and hitherto often isolated cultures of the world.

POINTS TO PONDER

1. Western imperialism extended its dominion over four-fifths of the globe.

2. Imperialism was a complex phenomenon in which motives of profit, power, and altruism were often mixed.

3. The result of Western imperialism was the beginning of an international culture.

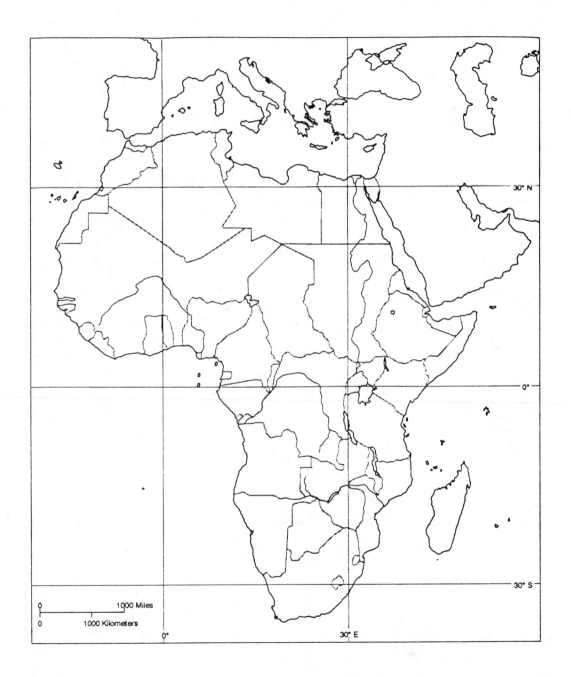

30° N

0°

30° S

0 1000 Miles

0 1000 Kilometers

0°

30° E

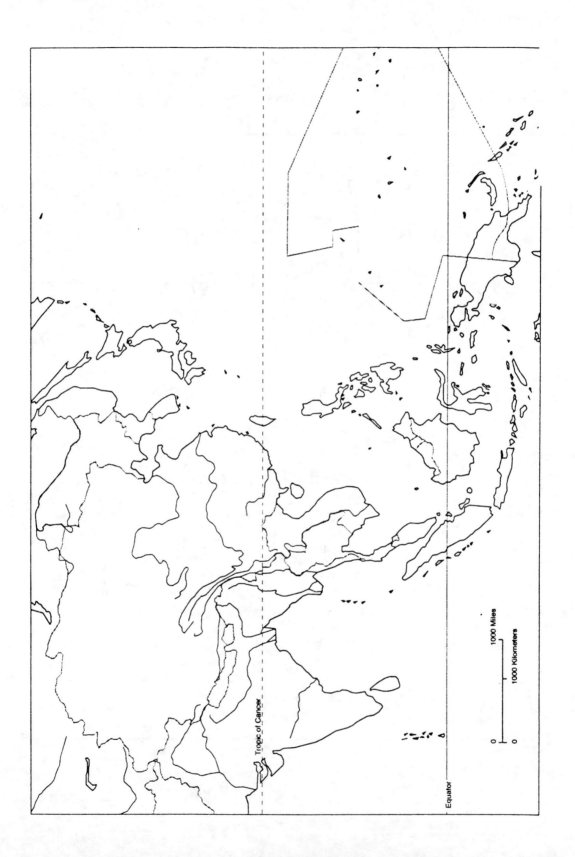

Tropic of Cancer

Equator

1000 Miles

1000 Kilometers

GEOGRAPHY

Locate the following on the first map:

Morocco   Sudan
Algeria   Ethiopia
Tunisia   French West Africa
Libya   French Equatorial Africa
Egypt   Cameroon

Locate the following on the second map:

Oudh   Burma
Rangoon   Siam (Thailand)
Bangkok   Singapore
Malaya   Penang
Sumatra   Java

1. Why did Britain's imperial holdings give it a commanding position in the Indian Ocean and the South China Sea?

2. Why did Russia's geographical position make it a major competitor of Britain's in Asia?

CHRONOLOGY

Number the following in correct chronological sequence:

1. _____ Berlin Conference

2. _____ Jameson Raid

3. _____ Boxer Rebellion

4. _____ Government of India Act

5. _____ Taiping Rebellion begins

6. _____ Amritsar Massacre

7. _____ Suez Canal opens

8. _____ Russo-Japanese War

9. _____ First colony in Australia

IDENTIFICATION

1. John A. Hobson

2. Mungo Park

3. Shaka

4. International Congo Association

5. New Delhi

6. Indian National Congress

7. Amritsar Massacre

8. Treaty ports

9. Taiping Rebellion

10. Fashoda

11. Cecil Rhodes

12. Maori

13. Ito Hirobumi

14. Twenty-one Demands

15. Battle of Adowa

DEFINITION

1. New Imperialism

2. Surplus capital

3. "White man's burden"

4. "Civil lines"

5. Extraterritoriality

6. Gunboat diplomacy

7. Great Trek

8. "Self-strengthening"

COMPLETION

1. The Belgian Congo was privately ruled by _____.

2. The Dutch farmers who settled southern Africa in the seventeenth century were called

   the _____.

3. The only African state to successfully resist colonization in the nineteenth century was

   _____.

4. The Dual System of government was abolished in India in the wake of

   _____.

5. The agreements that forced trade and other concessions on China and Japan were

   known as the _____.

6. Chinese who attended Western church services in return for handouts were known as

   _____.

7. Japan's first conquest in Asia was _____.

8. Japan's investment in _____ laid the basis for China's industrialization after 1945.

9. The first settlers in Australia were largely _____.

10. The French empire in Asia was centered in _____.

SHORT ANSWER

1. How did Lenin interpret the West's scramble for colonies?

2. What role was played by missionaries in Western imperialism?

3. What were the underlying causes of the Boer War?

4. How did Britain rule India after the Mutiny of 1857?

5. What role did ethnic Chinese play in the colonial regimes of Southeast Asia?

6. How did the treaties imposed on China by the great powers infringe on its sovereignty?

7.   What were the causes and consequences of the Taiping Rebellion?

8.   What steps did Japan take to modernize itself in the wake of the Meiji Restoration?

9.   What steps did Japan take in its attempt to become the dominant power in China?

10. How did British imperial policy in Australia and New Zealand differ from that adopted elsewhere in Asia?

UNDERSTANDING THE DOCUMENTS

1.   How do Hobson and Lenin differ from recent analysts in their approach to imperialism?

2.   How were arbitrary violence and terror used in extracting the forced labor of native populations in central Africa?

3.   What does Livingstone's account of tribal custom in Africa reveal about the relative positions of wives, mothers, and matriarchs? How real is the female dominance he claims to discern?

4.   How does the Chinese official's letter reveal China's continuing illusions about the outside world on the eve of the Opium War?

5.   How do these very different definitions of arrogance and conceit reveal the gulf that separated China from its foreign exploiters?

TERM-PAPER TOPICS

Interpretations of Imperialism
Economic Causes of Empire
Heart of Darkness: Leopold and the Belgian Congo
The Good Imperialist: David Livingstone
Cecil Rhodes: Empire–builder
The Scramble for Africa: Causes and Consequences
Colonial Life in India
The Growth of Indian Nationalism
China Besieged: The Imperial Powers and the Celestial Throne
The Boxer Rebellion
Tz'u Hsi, the Dowager Empress
The Modernization of Japan
The Dark Valley: Japanese Imperialism in Asia
Fables of Empire: E. M. Forster's *A Passage to India* and George Orwell's *Burmese Days*
White Islands: The Settling of Australia and New Zealand

CHAPTER 36

CULTURE, SOCIETY, AND THE GREAT WAR

OUTLINE

Society and Culture: The Impact of War
    Social Change and Economic Crisis
    The New Morality: Women, Work, and Sex
    Josephine Baker: An American in Paris
    Science, Literature, and Art

OVERVIEW

The Great War is in many ways the crucial event of the modern West. It shattered Western hegemony, stimulating the nationalist movements in India and elsewhere that would result in the abandonment of European empire forty years later and shifting the balance of world power toward the United States and Japan. It created upheaval in Russia, culminating in the establishment of a Bolshevik state whose revolutionary ambitions were a challenge to the capitalist order everywhere. It substantially redrew the map of Europe, and brought a host of new nations into being. Dictatorial regimes emerged in its aftermath in much of southern and eastern Europe, and totalitarian governments emerged in Italy and Germany.

The war was preceded by a long period of political and cultural crisis. Traditional positivism was challenged by the antirationalist philosophies of Nietzsche and Bergson, the psychoanalytic theories of Freud and Jung, the quantum mechanics of Planck, and the relativity of Einstein. The arts witnessed a similar rebellion against realism, in literature with Decadence and Symbolism, and in painting with Impressionism, Postimpressionism, and Cubism. More disturbingly, the age of mass politics was ushered in with new theories about crowd psychology and the need for elites to lead them, and with racially-based notions of national "character." The latter were often overtly anti-Semitic, as the Jews of Europe were subjected to persecution ranging from the Dreyfus affair in France to the pogroms of Russia.

As irrationalist theories of culture and race gained ground, the Concert of Europe collapsed under the strain of new political alignments. The Continent gradually divided into rival alliance systems in the wake of German and Italian unification, eroding the great power consensus that had controlled interstate conflict. An unchecked arms race, global economic and imperial competition, and the collapse of Ottoman authority in the Balkans led through a series of crises to war following the assassination of the Archduke Franz Ferdinand in June 1914.

The outbreak of war confounded all expectations of a brief, decisive campaign. Military technology enforced a deadly stalemate in which no advantage was to be had except by sheer attrition. As the human cost of the war mounted, victory alone could justify the sacrifice, creating a diplomatic deadlock as profound as the military one. The balance was finally tipped by the entry of the last major nonbelligerent, the United States, on the side of the Allies. The war's end, with more than 10 million dead, brought no sense of triumph to the victors. On all sides, there was consciousness that the war had shaken Western civilization to its core, and weakened European dominion around the globe. Revolution in Russia was followed by abortive uprisings in Germany and Hungary. The mobilization of society in the interests of "total" war paved the way for totalitarian governments, while gender controls were weakened, at least temporarily, by the mass entry of women into the labor force.

The world that emerged from the Great War was no more secure than the one that had preceded it. The Paris Peace Conference produced a harsh and vindictive treaty designed to cripple defeated Germany, while Austria-Hungary was dismembered, creating a vacuum of power in central and eastern Europe. The 1920s were characterized by a restless search for "collective security," but the threat of economic crisis hovered over the decade. The postwar art of the "Lost Generation" reflected social fracture and the influence of Freudian theory, while science moved from Einstein's relativity theory to Heisenberg's uncertainty principle as it gradually abandoned the hope of offering a coherent picture of the physical world. Women retained at least some of the occupational and sexual freedom they had won during the war, as symbolized by the career of Josephine Baker, but this too was seen by conservatives as a symptom of degeneracy, and a pretext for totalitarian repression in the years to come.

POINTS TO PONDER

1. The Great War was perhaps the major turning point in the history of the modern West.

2. The outbreak of the war was preceded by a long period of political and cultural crisis.

3. The war weakened the West both internally and externally, paving the way for worldwide revolts against the European order and for the rise of totalitarian regimes on the Continent itself.

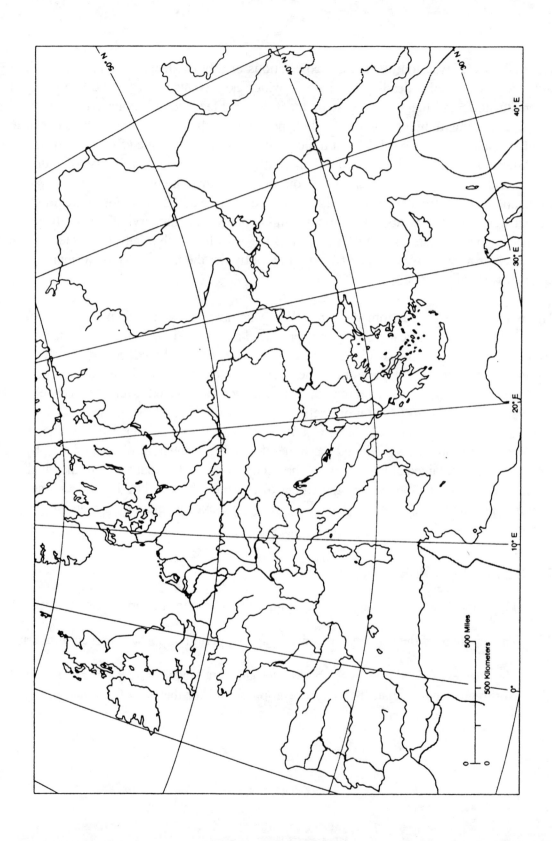

500 Miles

500 Kilometers

GEOGRAPHY

Locate the following on the map:

Ypres
Somme River
Marne River
Verdun
Rhine River
Jutland
Caporetto
Tannenberg
Brest-Litovsk
Sarajevo
Serbia
Tyrol
Fiume
Alsace

Lorraine
Versailles
Saar region
Weimar
Austria
Czechoslovakia
Hungary
Poland
Yugoslavia
Romania
Lithuania
Latvia
Estonia
Soviet Union

1.   What territorial losses did Germany suffer as a result of World War I?

2.   Why did eastern Europe remain unstable after World War I?

CHRONOLOGY

Number the following in correct chronological sequence:

1. _____ Treaty of Versailles

2. _____ Einstein's "Special Theory of Relativity"

3. _____ Baudelaire's *Flowers of Evil*

4. _____ Formation of the Triple Alliance

5. _____ First Balkan War

6. _____ Locarno Pact

7. _____ Balfour Declaration

8. _____ First Cubist paintings exhibited

9. _____ Sinking of the *Lusitania*

IDENTIFICATION

1. Friedrich Nietzsche

2. Sigmund Freud

3. Stéphane Mallarmé

4.   Antonio Gaudí

5.   Fauvism

6.   T. E. Lawrence

7.   Battle of Verdun

8.   Edith Cavell

9.   Fourteen Points

10. Ernest Rutherford

11. Georges Clemenceau

12. Article 231

13. Luigi Pirandello

14. Josephine Baker

15. Kellogg-Briand Pact

DEFINITION

1. Id

2. "Special Theory of Relativity"

3. Postimpressionism

4. Futurism

5. Mandate principle

6. Logical Positivism

7.   Lost Generation

8.   Bauhaus

COMPLETION

1.   The empires that disappeared as a result of the Great War were _____

_____.

2.   Nietzsche called his ideal hero _____.

3.   The reactionary political organization founded by the French monarchist Charles

Maurras was the _____.

4.   Richard Wagner's famous operatic cycle is _____.

5.   Britain ended its diplomatic isolation in 1902 with an agreement with

_____.

6.   William II's assurance of unqualified support for Austria-Hungary after the

assassination of Franz Ferdinand became known as the _____.

7.   After World War I, the United States rejected participation in the

_____ _____.

8. France's postwar alliance with Poland, Romania, and Yugoslavia was known as the

    _____.

9. D. H. Lawrence's controversial novel _____ was

    censored for its explicit description of sexual desire.

10. An historian's prediction of Europe's decay was Oswald Spengler's _____

    _____.

SHORT ANSWER

1. Why was Bismarck's alliance with Austria-Hungary and Europe a fateful step for
    Europe?

2. How did racism affect nationalism in the late nineteenth century?

3. How did Sigmund Freud's theories reflect the new emphasis on the irrational in
    European culture?

4. How was Symbolism a reaction against the values and assumptions of positivism?

5. How was the displacement of time and space in Cubist art related to scientific
    developments such as Einstein's theory of relativity?

6. How did military conscription and the arms race affect the climate of Europe in the years before World War I?

7. Why did the United States enter World War I after three years of neutrality?

8. Why did the victorious Allies insist on formally blaming Germany for World War I at the Versailles Conference?

9. How was the position of women affected by the Great War?

10. How did the art of postwar Europe reflect a quest for new meaning in the aftermath of devastation?

UNDERSTANDING THE DOCUMENTS

1. How does Marinetti's manifesto reflect a rejection of traditional values in favor of those associated with the new industrial society?

2. How do the descriptions of the British soldiers illustrate the dehumanizing effects of trench warfare?

3. How does Keynes' description of the Versailles Conference reflect the postwar atmosphere of Europe?

4. How does Ortega's description of the postwar world reflect the break between the complacency of nineteenth-century materialism and the trauma of the twentieth-century world?

TERM-PAPER TOPICS

Nietzsche and the Revolt Against Positivism
Racist Ideology in Prewar Europe
The Discovery of the Unconscious
From Impressionism to Cubism: The Birth of Modern Art
The Scandal of Oscar Wilde
The Foreign Policy of Bismarck
The Alliance System and the Breakdown of Diplomacy
The New Physics
The Fischer Thesis and the Outbreak of World War I
Life in the Trenches
Wilson, American Opinion, and the Rejection of the League of Nations
The Sexual Revolution
Josephine Baker and the Jazz Age
The Quest for Postwar Stability
Censorship and Literature: *Ulysses* and *Lady Chatterley's Lover*

GLOBAL ESSAY

THE HUMAN IMAGE (II)

OVERVIEW

The sixteenth century brought a more secular and more personalized view of the human image to many cultures, notably those of Europe and India. Artists themselves, such as Michelangelo, became culture heroes, and the growth of both private and political patronage helped shift the focus of art away from purely religious themes. The human figure became increasingly important in Japanese art as well, where woodblock prints fed a popular appetite for representations of exotic personages and entertainers. In Africa, masks and carvings depicted the human form in a wide range of styles. Only in China did the older landscape tradition persist.

The art of Renaissance Europe, itself inspired by classical antiquity, set the standard of physical beauty until the nineteenth century. Among Renaissance genres, the individual portrait and the female nude (often treated symbolically or allegorically) remained particularly popular. Encounters with the art of other cultures helped stimulate a radical shift in artistic style in the later nineteenth century, with Japanese prints strongly influencing Impressionist and Postimpressionist painters, and African masks the Cubism of Picasso.

Twentieth-century art reflected a crisis in portraying the human image. Styles such as Expressionism and Surrealism reflected the influence of Freudian psychology and the traumatic experience of World War I, while Abstract Expressionism, pioneered by Kandinsky, moved beyond the representation of recognizable forms altogether. The attempt to depict idealized "Aryan" figures in Nazi propaganda backfired; the masterpieces of nonrepresentational art continued to draw admiring crowds. The human image could return to art only on its own terms. Pop Art, with images derived from popular forms such as advertising and the comic strip, restored the human form in the 1960s, while a new generation of artists, including Anselm Kiefer, returned to it to depict German cultural history in the light of the Nazi experience.

IDENTIFICATION

1. Giorgio Vasari

2. Benin art

3. Titian

4. *St. Theresa in Ecstasy*

5. Ukiyo-e

6. Mughal art

7. Paul Cézanne

8. Expressionism

COMPLETION

1. The _____ of Florence were important secular patrons of the Renaissance.

2. The art of the portrait miniature was exquisitely developed at the court of _____.

3. Japanese art of the eighteenth century reflected the interests and lifestyles of an emerging _____.

4. For an ideal representation of the female nude, Renaissance painters looked back to the figure of _____.

5. The spiritual values of the Counter-Reformation were represented in the work of the _____.

6. The French Revolution is glorified in David's _____.

7. A distorted figure in an echoing landscape is the theme of Edvard Munch's _____.

8. Cults of personality were satirized in _____.

SHORT ANSWER

1. How did patronage by secular rulers affect representations of the human image in the sixteenth century?

2. How did the types and purposes of representation of Japanese art change with the shift from scroll to print as a primary means of expression?

3. Why has relatively little African art survived from the period before the arrival of Western explorers?

4. How does the work of Donatello and Da Vinci combine both Christian and secular concerns?

5. How does baroque art reflect the preoccupation with the struggle between spirit and flesh?

6. How was late nineteenth-century and twentieth-century Western art influenced by the art of other cultures?

7. How have modern political regimes attempted to manipulate the representation of the human figure in art?

TERM-PAPER TOPICS

The Renaissance and the Classical Ideal
Art and Patronage in Renaissance Italy
The Artist as Culture Hero since the Renaissance
The Mughal Miniature
The Mask in African Art
The Japanese Print and Its Influence
Art and Anxiety: The Human Image from Expressionism to Surrealism
Pop Art and After: The Human Image in Our Time

CHAPTER 37

UPHEAVAL IN EURASIA AND THE MIDDLE EAST

OUTLINE

OVERVIEW

The first half of the twentieth century was marked by major upheavals in China, Russia, India, and the Middle East, together involving half of the world's population. National identity, independence from foreign control, and the quest for social justice marked the struggles in each region; each as well dealt with the demands of modernization and their often painful impact on traditional culture.

The Russian Revolution was the direct result of World War I, which overwhelmed the tsarist autocracy. The Bolshevik state it finally produced was the outcome of decisive and ruthless action by a small determined group at a moment of crisis and anarchy. Once established, Bolshevism was able to stave off internal opposition and outside intervention by appeals to patriotism, promises of reform, and skillful military action. The devastation of world war, civil war, and famine obliged the Bolshevik leader, Lenin, to pause in his plans to collectivize Russian society, but his successor, Stalin, moved quickly to institute full control over the economy. Within a decade, the framework of a totalitarian society had been imposed on what was now called the Union of Soviet Socialist Republics.

The Chinese Revolution was less clearcut. The fall of the Ch'ing dynasty in 1911 was little more than a garrison revolt, and it was by no means evident that a new dynasty would not emerge, as so had often before. With the warlord Yuan Shih-kai's failure to be proclaimed emperor, however, the ideological balance of the revolution returned to its most prominent figure, Sun Yat-sen, an eclectic Westernizer and admirer of Lenin. His successor Chiang Kai-shek was able to create a measure of stability by allying his own nationalist (Kuomintang) party with Communist insurgents. The alliance proved temporary, and Chiang's essentially reactionary outlook, combined with the shock of Japanese invasion, would postpone the final settlement of the revolution until after World War II.

In India, nationalist energies were concentrated on the goal of winning independence from Britain. Britain's military control of the subcontinent dictated the tactics of nonviolent mass action so skillfully employed by Gandhi, who was ultimately able to force the British to honor the commitment they had made in 1907 to Indian independence. As in China, the process was painfully prolonged, and disputes between Hindus and Muslims would result in the division of British India into three and eventually four separate entities, India, Pakistan, Sri Lanka, and Bangladesh.

The Middle East was a theater of war during World War I, with British and French interests pitted against an emerging Arab nationalism for control of the former Ottoman Empire. A complex series of events led to nationalist revolution in Turkey and the establishment of the desert kingdom of Saudi Arabia and the Pahlavi dynasty in Iran, with Western protectorates dominating the rest of the region. The promise of a Jewish homeland in the Balfour Declaration added a deeply complicating factor to the equation—the recognition of Zionist nationalism in Palestine. As in India and China, World War II was followed by a bloody climax to these events.

POINTS TO PONDER

1. Internal revolutions and nationalist struggles for independence affected half the world's population during the first half of the twentieth century.

2. In Russia and China, revolution led to the overthrow of traditional dynasties and the In India and the establishment of totalitarian regimes.

3. Middle East, Western influence was challenged or overthrown as new states emerged and others threw off colonial domination.

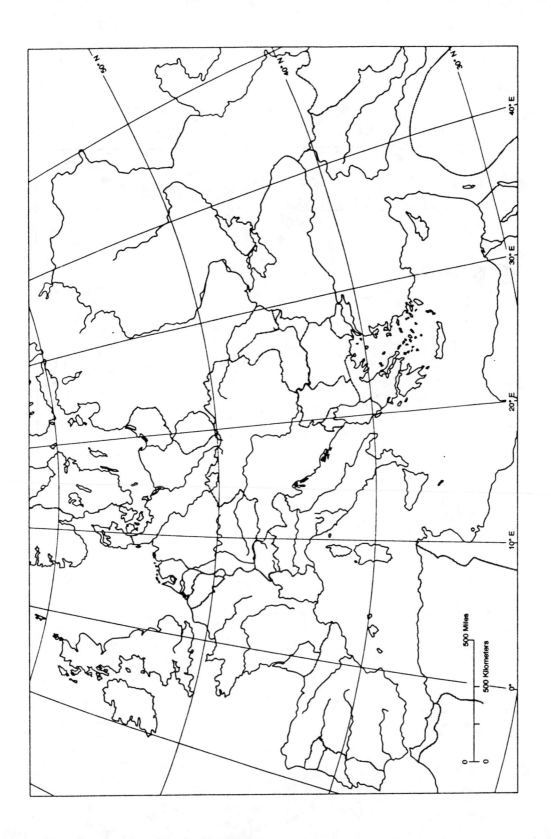

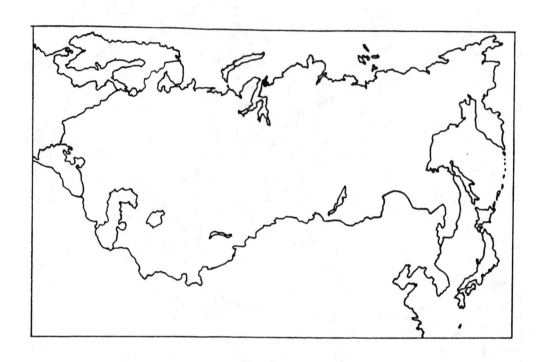

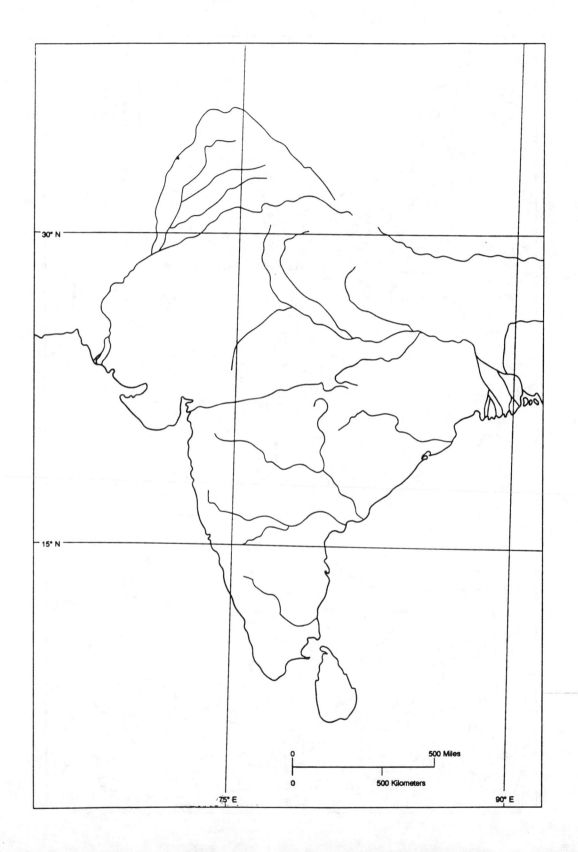

30° N

15° N

0   500 Miles

0   500 Kilometers

75° E   90° E

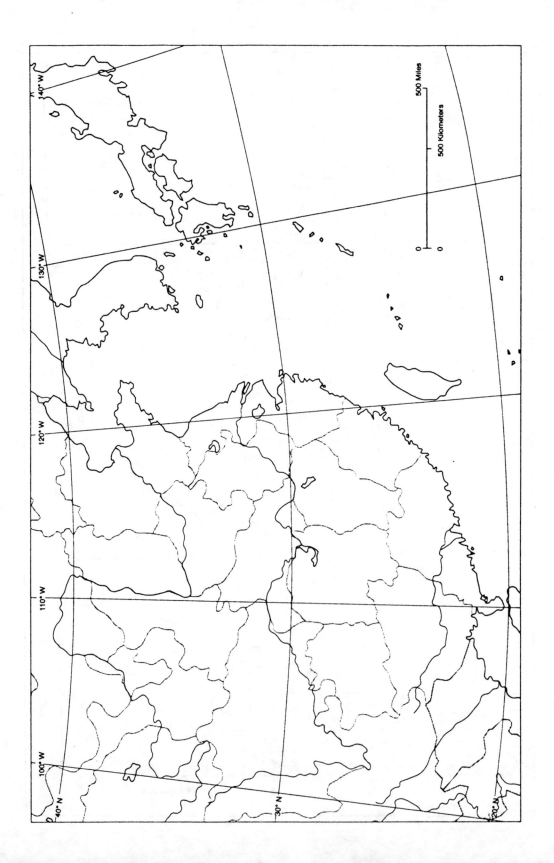

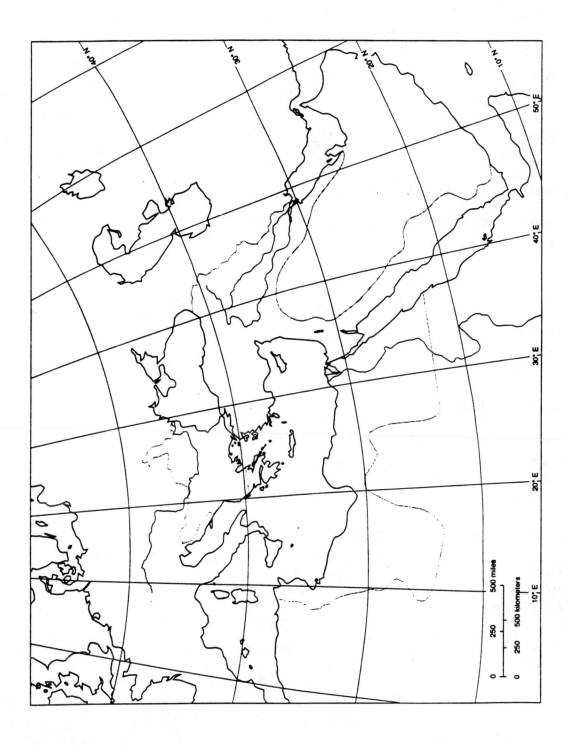

GEOGRAPHY

Locate the following on the first map:

Petrograd	Crimea
Kronstadt	Black Sea
Moscow	Georgia
Brest-Litovsk	Caspian Sea
Archangel	

Locate the following on the second map:

Vladivostok	Caspian Sea
Black Sea	Archangel

Locate the following on the third map:

Karachi	Bombay
Madras	Calcutta
Delhi	Ceylon (Sri Lanka)
Himalayas	

Locate the following on the fourth map:

Peking	Canton
Mukden	Taiwan
Dairen	Yenan
Shanghai	Hong Kong

Locate the following on the fifth map:

Turkey	Lebanon
Syria	Palestine
Transjordan	Iraq
Iran	Saudi Arabia
Persian Gulf	Red Sea
Egypt	

1. How did the long frontier between Russia and China affect their revolutionary experience?

2. Why did the division of British India into India and Pakistan create geographical friction between the two states?

CHRONOLOGY

Number the following in correct chronological sequence:

1. _____ Communist International disbanded

2. _____ May Fourth movement in China

3. _____ Gandhi leads protest march against the salt tax

4. _____ Lenin announces his New Economic Policy

5. _____ Balfour Declaration

6. _____ Trotsky goes into exile

7. _____ Mao's Long March

8. _____ India gains independence

9. _____ Young Turks seize power

IDENTIFICATION

1. 1905 Revolution

2. Alexander Kerensky

3. April Theses

4. Comintern

5. Alexandra Kollontai

6. Sun Yat-sen

7. Three Principles of the People

8. Kuomintang

9. Mao Tse-tung

10. Jawaharlal Nehru

11. Ali Jinnah

12. "Quit India" movement

13. Sykes-Picot Agreement

14. Chaim Weizmann

15. Kemal Atatürk

DEFINITION

1. Duma

2. War Communism

3. Permanent Revolution

4. May Fourth movement

5. Long March

6. Yishuv

7. Young Turks

COMPLETION

1. The tsar overthrown by the Russian Revolution was _____.

2. The Marxist party in Russia was divided into two factions, _____

   and _____.

3. "Socialism in one country" was the slogan of _____.

4. China was dominated in the early years of its revolution by regional chieftains called

   _____.

5. After 1910 the largest city in China was _____.

6. Traditional Chinese society was denounced by the writer _____.

7. The turning point in the Indian independence movement was the _____ _____.

8. Gandhi based his tactics on the ancient Hindu idea of _____ or reverence for life.

9. An Arab congress declared King _____ ruler of Syria, Palestine, and Lebanon after World War I.

10. Many Jewish settlers in Palestine performed collective agricultural labor on a farm unit known as the _____.

SHORT ANSWER

1. What were the major factors behind the Russian Revolution of March 1917?

2. How were the Bolsheviks, a small party with little following in early 1917, able to seize control of Russia by November?

3. How did Lenin adapt his tactics to the changing circumstances of the Revolution?

4. How was Stalin able to prevail over Trotsky in the struggle for power after Lenin's death?

5. Why was China unable to consolidate after the 1911 revolution?

6. Why was the government of Chiang Kai-shek ultimately a failure?

7. Why was the granting of independence so long delayed in India?

8. How were Gandhi's revolutionary tactics adapted to the conditions of both Indian culture and British rule?

9. How did the collapse of the Ottoman Empire lead to the rise of competing nationalisms?

10. How did the Western powers attempt to exploit the mandate system in the Middle East?

UNDERSTANDING THE DOCUMENTS

1. How does Lenin understand the relationship between leaders and masses in a revolutionary struggle?

2. How does Trotsky justify the suffering caused by revolution?

3. How does the exchange between Lenin and Roy illustrate the tensions within the Comintern?

4. How does Gandhi illustrate his revolutionary strategy in his address to the English?

5. How does Nehru's declaration of Indian freedom echo Western ideas of self-determination as it rejects British domination?

TERM-PAPER TOPICS

The Fall of the Romanov Dynasty
The Provisional Government: Russia's Failed Liberal Experiment
Red versus White: The Russian Civil War
Lenin and the Left Opposition to Communism
Stalin: The Rise of a Dictator
Sun Yat-sen and the Chinese Revolution of 1911
The May Fourth Movement and Modernization in China
The Kuomintang in Power
Russian Influence in the Chinese Revolution
Mao and the Long March
Amritsar: The Massacre and Its Consequences
Gandhi's Philosophy of Nonviolence
Gandhi and Jinnah: The Struggle for Control of the Indian Independence Movement
Arab and Jew in Mandate Palestine
T. E. Lawrence and the Genesis of Arab Nationalism
Iran and the West

CHAPTER 38

TOTALITARIANISM AND THE CRISIS OF DEMOCRACY

OUTLINE

OVERVIEW

World War I, Woodrow Wilson proclaimed, was fought to make the world safe for democracy. At the end of the war, democratic regimes were installed in the successor states of Eastern Europe, and the Weimar Republic assumed power in Germany. Within twenty years these regimes had all vanished, to be replaced by authoritarian if not totalitarian governments, mostly of a military or monarchist stamp. Democracy was shaken though not displaced in Britain, France, and the United States, as the Great Depression called into question the assumptions of liberal capitalism, and the ability of parliamentary regimes to cope with widespread suffering and unrest. The larger democracies rode out the storm with economic controls, protectionism, reflation schemes, and the abandonment of the gold standard, but at serious cost to living standards and world trade.

Beyond economic malaise, the democracies were subject to a more fundamental challenge by the postwar rise of fascist regimes, which many felt represented the only viable alternative between Communism and democracy. Fascism was a form of totalitarianism characterized by an appeal to nationalism and personal sacrifice, the glorification of militarism and violence, the exaltation of a leader supposedly embodying the will of the people, and the alleged transcendence of class and party interests. It offered a unitary view of society as dominated by the state, in which all civil pursuits were authorized by the state and subordinated to its ends. Propaganda, mass activity, and control of education were the means employed to mobilize the population; surveillance and terror were used to crush dissent.

Fascism rested on no clearly articulated theory, as did Communism. It flourished best where democratic institutions were weak, parliamentary governments divided, and social forces polarized. Its prototype was Mussolini's Italy, where his Fascist Party bluffed its way into power in 1922 following a series of political crises, evolved by stages into a totalitarian regime, and retained an air of improvisation almost to the end. It exhibited nonetheless the major characteristics of fascism: a supreme leader and a one-party state; suppression of independent power centers; coordination of economic activity and control of labor; propaganda, mass rallies, and obligatory displays of loyalty; militarism and imperialism. As elsewhere, Italian Fascism worked through a shrewd conciliation of the elites, in Italy's case including the industrial bourgeoisie, the landowning class, and the church.

The Nazi movement in Germany came to power in 1933 under the leadership of Adolf Hitler, who called his regime the Third Reich to signify his break with the immediate German past. Nazism borrowed many of its tactics and much of its ideology from Mussolini, but added two distinctive elements: racism and anticlericalism. Nazi racism—the idea of a German master race—derived from extreme nineteenth-century ideologies of nationalism and imperialism, mixed with traditional anti-Semitism. It was integral to the Hitler regime, providing both a pretext for totalitarian controls at home and a policy of conquest abroad. Anticlericalism also helped clear the path for a total monopoly of power by the state. Whereas Italian Fascism was partly mitigated by Mussolini's need to deal with the Catholic church, Hitler had no such constraint, and his feared secret police, the Gestapo, became a byword for terror. He targeted deviant groups such as homosexuals and alleged racial inferiors such as gypsies, but his most systematic persecution was reserved for the Jews, beginning with the removal of their citizenship and the confiscation of their property and resulting ultimately in the attempt to exterminate the entire Jewish population of the European continent.

Other varieties of fascism developed in Belgium, Romania, and Austria, a fascist government gained power in Spain under General Francisco Franco after a three-year civil war, and quasi-fascist regimes emerged in Japan and Brazil. Significant fascist movements also appeared in Britain and France, where there was open admiration for Italy and Germany among some elite elements in the 1930s (as in the United States as well). At the same time, fascism appealed to many underdeveloped regions as a solution to the problems of modernization, just as state-directed "socialism" would in the postcolonial period after World War II. Alliances between fascist states were problematic, however, since each stressed competitive nationalism. Mussolini blocked a union between Germany and Austria in 1934, and his later alliance with Hitler reflected more the latter's dominance than any community of interest. Nonetheless, fascism seemed to be gaining ground in the 1930s as rapidly as the democracies were losing it, and many saw in it, in the words of Anne Morrow Lindbergh, the "wave of the future."

A different but no less oppressive totalitarianism developed in the Soviet Union, where the state's domination of the social order was enhanced by its monopoly of capital. Lenin had seized control of the major industries and utilities of Russia, and although he had permitted a market economy to function in the 1920s, Stalin moved rapidly to implement a planned system after 1928, including the forced collectivization of agriculture. These measures were enforced by the systematic starvation of millions and the removal of millions of others to forced labor camps. Industry was built up through a series of five-year plans that diverted all available capital and produced a severe depression of living standards and, in the Ukraine, actual famine. This was partially compensated by health and pension benefits, free education, subsidized housing, and wider economic opportunities for women. As in Italy and Germany, the leader was relentlessly glorified and dissent was met with imprisonment and death. In the late 1930s Stalin instituted a series of purges that engulfed high-ranking party members, bureaucrats, and army officers, and swept up millions into death or exile.

POINTS TO PONDER

1. Democracies were established in the former empires of Germany and Austria and the new states of eastern Europe after World War I, but they were entirely swept away in the next twenty years.

2. Fascism was a form of totalitarianism based on state monopoly of power, aggressive nationalism, and a one-party system dominated by a single leader.

3. Despite differences of ideology, both the fascist regimes in Italy and Germany and the Soviet regime in Russia were totalitarian societies that demanded complete submission to the state.

CHRONOLOGY

Number the following in correct chronological sequence:

1. _____ Franklin D. Roosevelt becomes President

2. _____ Mussolini's march on Rome

3. _____ Failure of the *Creditanstalt* in Austria

4. _____ General strike in Britain

5. _____ Vargas comes to power in Brazil

6. _____ Popular Front government in France

7. _____ Weimar Republic established in Germany

8. _____ First Five-Year Plan begins in the Soviet Union

9. _____ Munich Beer Hall Putsch

IDENTIFICATION

1. Gabriele D'Annunzio

2. Spartacists

3. Free Corps

4.   Iron Guard

5.   Sir Oswald Mosley

6.   Bertolt Brecht

7.   Kita Ikki

8.   Margin trading

9.   Collectivization

10.   Joseph Goebbels

11.   Falange

12.   Ramsay MacDonald

13. "Old Bolsheviks"

14. Estado Novo

15. Croix de Feu

DEFINITION

1. Successor states

2. Great Depression

3. New Deal

4. Popular Front

5. Weimar Republic

6. Schutzstaffel (SS)

7. Great Purges

8. Integralismo

COMPLETION

1. Many people in the interwar period saw fascism as a third way between _____ and _____ .

2. The mass base of fascism came chiefly from the _____ .

3. The first attempt to topple the Weimar Republic was the _____

    _____ .

4. Hitler set out his political philosophy in _____ .

5. The dramatic style developed by Brecht was called _____ .

6. The _____ were a group of young military officers who

    demanded modernization in Brazil.

7. Jews were deprived of their citizenship in Germany by _____ .

8. The founder of the Falangist movement was _____ .

9. Stalin's purges began with the assassination of _____ .

10. The Great Depression in the United States was triggered by _____ .

SHORT ANSWER

1. What were the major characteristics of fascism as a political system?

2. How did fascism differ from communism?

3.   How did the postwar climate of Italy help make Fascism possible?

4.   In what ways did Nazism differ from Italian Fascism?

5.   Why was democracy unable to maintain itself in the successor states?

6.   What were the fascist characteristics of Vargas' Estado Novo in Brazil?

7.   What was the impact of the Great Depression on the liberal democracies?

8.   What were the measures by which totalitarian regimes crushed dissent?

9.   What was the human cost of Stalin's programs of industrialization and collectivization in the Soviet Union?

UNDERSTANDING THE DOCUMENTS

1. How does Mussolini's speech define the role of the state in Italian Fascism?

2. How did Speer connect Hitler's personal psychology and political ideology with his plans to redesign Berlin?

3. How does Hitler's view of history as a struggle between contending individuals and groups serve to justify his declared policy of aggression?

4. Which themes of Italian and German fascism are echoed in Vargas' description of the Brazilian Estado Novo?

TERM-PAPER TOPICS

Interpretations of Fascism
Mussolini's Socialist Period
The Consolidation of Fascist Power in Italy
Fascism and the Churches
The Fascist System of Terror
Fascist Propaganda: Creating the Big Lie
Fascism and Women
Fascism and Militarism in Japan
Fascism in the New World
The Theater of Bertolt Brecht
The Totalitarian Cult of Personality
Collectivizing Soviet Russia: Costs and Consequences
Stalin's Reign of Terror
The Causes of the Great Depression
Coping with the Crash: Britain, France, and the United States
The Weimar Republic
The Failure of East European Democracy

CHAPTER 39

THE SECOND WORLD WAR TO THE COLD WAR

OUTLINE

OVERVIEW

The roots of World War II lay in the Great War and the divisive peace settlements that followed it. The failure of collective leadership and the rise of totalitarian dictatorships led to a revival of militant nationalism in Europe, while Japan sought to replace the Western presence in Asia with its own regional empire. The result was a new global conflict that, unfolding on a vast scale both in Europe and Asia, eclipsed even World War I in its devastation.

The road to a new world war began in Japan, which, although it lacked the formal trappings of a fascist state, was a highly regimented society dominated by a military and industrial elite. Having occupied the Chinese province of Manchuria, it launched a full-scale attack on China in 1937 as the initial step in its planned domination of the Far East. The failure of the former Allied powers to check Japan's first acts of aggression emboldened Mussolini to conquer Ethiopia and Hitler to rearm and reoccupy the Rhineland, while the neutrality of the democracies doomed the republican cause in Spain in the face of a fascist revolt. The climax of appeasement, as the French and British policy came to be called, occurred with Hitler's occupation of Austria and Czechoslovakia. Thereafter, Britain and France reluctantly prepared for war, only to face the full force of Nazi Germany when Hitler and Stalin signed a nonaggression pact in August 1939. With the invasion of Poland a week later, World War II began.

A year after the war's outbreak, Japan joined Germany and Italy in the so-called Axis alliance, while with Hitler's attack on the Soviet Union in June 1941 and the Japanese bombing of Pearl Harbor in December, the old Allied alliance of World War I was reconstituted. Hitler's legions swept across Europe, not to be dislodged until Soviet forces drove the Nazis back after a titanic struggle and the Western Allies invaded occupied

France. The European war ended in 1945 with the conquest of Italy and Germany and the deaths of Hitler and Mussolini, and the Pacific war with the dropping of atomic bombs on the Japanese cities of Hiroshima and Nagasaki. To the more than 40 million lives lost among combatants and civilians alike was added the six million Jews who perished in Nazi extermination camps. As at the end of World War I, a new body, the United Nations, was established by the victors to promote international order.

The period after World War II was dominated by the rivalry between the two superpowers that emerged from it, the United States and the Soviet Union. The Soviets, having occupied eastern Europe during the war, remained to install a series of "people's democracies" in Poland, Hungary, Romania, Bulgaria, Czechoslovakia, Yugoslavia, and Albania, while following the establishment of the German Federal Republic (West Germany) in the Allied sectors of occupied Germany, they created a new state in their own sector, the German Democratic Republic (East Germany). Through coercive military and economic alliances, they incorporated the 90 million people of the region into a unitary bloc under their control.

The formation of the Soviet bloc was in part a response to America's initiatives in western Europe, NATO and the Marshall Plan, and in part a scheme to divert the region's wealth to the task of reconstructing the Soviet Union. Stalin's intention to create a security zone in eastern Europe, however, had been clear from the beginning. Only in Yugoslavia did a resourceful leader, Marshal Tito, successfully defy Moscow and establish an independent though nominally Communist regime. Elsewhere, overt resistance was crushed by the Red Army, notably in East Germany (1953), Hungary (1956), and Czechoslovakia (1968). Internally, the Soviet Union underwent a gradual liberalization following Stalin's death in 1953. In 1956, Stalin's successor, Nikita Khrushchev, made a startling attack on him at the Twentieth Party Congress that signaled the end of one-person though not one-party rule. Khrushchev himself would be deposed by the Politburo in 1964 following a confrontation with the United States over the attempt to station Soviet missiles in Cuba. Under both Khrushchev and his successor, Leonid Brezhnev, the Soviet regime evolved into a collegial system in which the Party Secretary governed by consensus within the Politburo. Despite the exclusion of the public at large from the Party political process, Soviet women enjoyed far greater access to the professions than in the United States.

The reconstruction of western Europe through the Marshall Plan was spurred by the United States' need to reopen markets for its excess industrial capacity. Politically, the U.S. sponsored centrist Christian Democratic parties in Germany and Italy. In Britain, the

Labour Party government of Clement Attlee nationalized key industries and established a welfare state, but did not break with the framework of liberal capitalism. In France, the Fourth Republic was able to contain a large Communist Party within parliamentary constraints. With recovery, western Europe began to shape its own economic destiny through the Common Market, and France under Charles de Gaulle left NATO, pursued an independent foreign policy, and (like Britain) built up its own nuclear arsenal. When China joined the nuclear club in 1964, efforts were made to control the spread of atomic weapons, resulting in the Nuclear Non-Proliferation Treaty. The very need for such an agreement signaled the end of uncontested superpower hegemony and the emergence of polycentrism.

These new alignments, together with internal changes and a period of increased tensions that climaxed with the Cuban missile crisis, brought about the relaxation in superpower relations known as détente. The Soviet Union sought relief from the arms race to make modest improvements in civilian living standards, while the United States, following the Cold War backlash of the McCarthy period, became embroiled in an historic struggle over black civil rights and a protracted neocolonial war in Vietnam that tested the political and cultural foundations of the country and led (together with changing labor and family patterns) to a powerful movement for women's rights. The missile crisis shook both superpowers, and led directly to the first arms control agreement of the postwar period, the Nuclear Test-Ban Treaty. Other agreements followed, including the Helsinki Accords on human rights, despite the setbacks occasioned by the Soviet invasions of Czechoslovakia and Afghanistan.

From the beginning, so-called Third World nations, many of them newly independent, sought to avoid commitment to either superpower, a policy known as nonalignment. Nehru's India became its chief advocate in Asia and Africa, and took the lead in convening the first meeting of nonaligned states, the Bandung Conference, in 1955. At the same time Gamal Abdel Nasser defied the West by seizing control of the Suez Canal, setting the pattern later successfully adopted by other Middle Eastern states in nationalizing their oil resources and forming a cartel, OPEC, which exercised decisive political as well as economic leverage in the 1970s. In Asia, China's break with the Soviet bloc in 1959 and the formidable recovery of Japan, by the 1980s the world's second largest industrial power, made superpower contention peripheral if not irrelevant in the Far East.

POINTS TO PONDER

1. The glorification of violence, militarism, and state power in both Germany and Japan and the failure of collective security to contain aggression led Europe and Asia on the path to renewed war in the 1930s.

2. World War II, marked by systematic genocide, unprecedented destruction, and the introduction of atomic weapons, was the bloodiest conflict in history.

3. The Cold War, beginning with a struggle between the United States and the Soviet Union for control of postwar Europe, evolved into a worldwide competition for power.

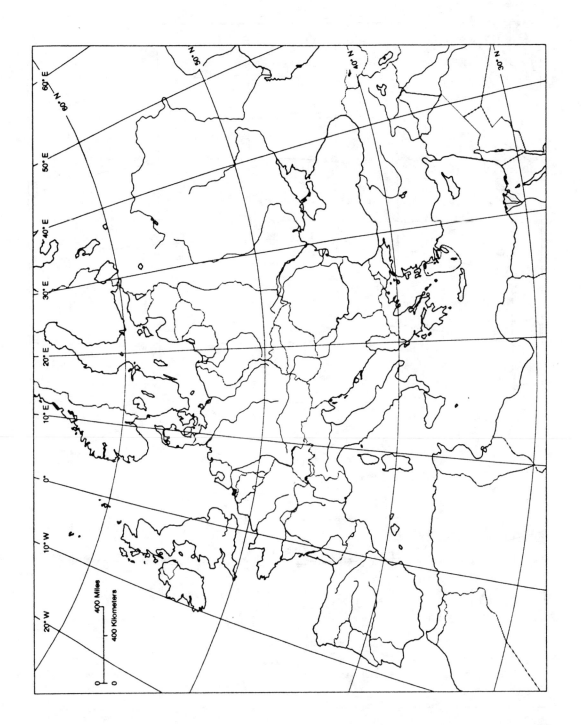

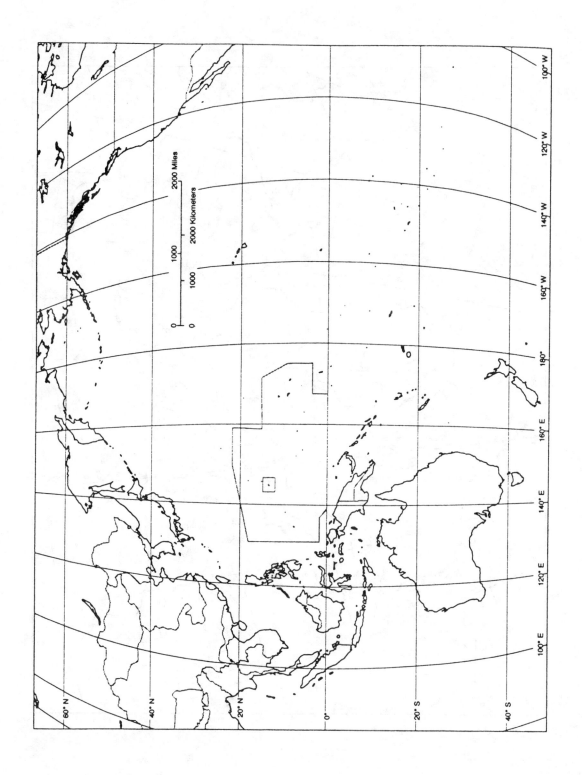

2000 Miles

2000 Kilometers

1000

1000

0

0

GEOGRAPHY

Locate the following on the first map:

London	Slovakia
Occupied France	Croatia
Vichy France	Serbia
Greater Germany	Sicily
Reich Protectorate of Bohemia	Ukraine
Austria	Stalingrad

Locate the following on the second map:

Japan	Manchuria (Manchukuo)
Okinawa	Iwo Jima
Philippines	New Guinea
Indochina	Burma
Korea	Shanghai
Nanking	Chungking

1. How does Hitler's empire at its height in 1942 compare with Napoleon's in 1812?

2. Why was naval power crucial to the determination of the Pacific war?

CHRONOLOGY

Number the following in correct chronological sequence:

1. _____ U.S. Congress passes the Equal Rights Amendment

2. _____ Nazi-Soviet Pact

3. _____ Japan invades Manchuria

4. _____ Founding of the United Nations

5. _____ Defeat of the German army at Stalingrad

6. _____ Margaret Thatcher becomes prime minister of Britain

7. _____ Khrushchev denounces Stalin's crimes at the Twentieth Party Congress

8. _____ Marshall Plan aid begins

9. _____ U.S. Supreme Court outlaws school segregation

IDENTIFICATION

1. Hiroshima

2. Neville Chamberlain

3. Berlin Blockade

4. Hungarian Revolution

5. NOW

6. *Blitzkrieg*

7. *Zaibatsu*

8. Konrad Adenauer

9. Atlantic Charter

10. War on Poverty

11. Subhas Chandra Bose

12. Fourth Republic (France)

13. Grand Alliance

14. Iron Curtain

15. Auschwitz

DEFINITION

1. Anschluss

2. Appeasement

3. Greater East Asian Co-Prosperity Sphere

4. Final Solution

5. Truman Doctrine

6. Brinkmanship

7. Ostpolitik

8. The Second Sex

COMPLETION

1. A major failure of the League of Nations was its inability to stop the Italian conquest of _____.

2. The alliance of the principal fascist powers was known as _____.

3. Britain and France agreed to the German occupation of the Sudetenland at the _____.

4. The leader of the Free French was _____.

5. The code name given to the development of the atomic bomb was _____.

6. The first open split between the United States and the Soviet Union occurred between Truman and Stalin at _____.

7. After World War II, surviving Nazi leaders were tried for war crimes by the _____.

8. The American-sponsored postwar military alliance in Europe was called _____.

9. The notion that people should take a greater part in the decisions that affect their lives was known in the 1960s as _____.

10. Communists who deviated from strict ideological orthodoxy were denounced as

_____.

SHORT ANSWER

1. What were Japan's goals and ambitions in Southeast Asia?

2. Why did Britain and France choose a policy of appeasement toward the fascist powers in the 1930s?

3. What were the purposes of Hitler and Stalin in signing their non-aggression pact?

4. Why did Chiang Kai-shek's prosecution of the war against Japan cost him the support of the Chinese people?

5. What considerations lay behind the United States' decision to use the atomic bomb?

6. Why did the United States take a more active international role after World War II than after World War I?

7. What were Stalin's primary goals in eastern Europe at the end of World War II?

8. What were the causes and consequences of McCarthyism in the United States?

9. What were the causes of disunity among the Communist powers after 1956?

10. What brought about the emergence of détente?

UNDERSTANDING THE DOCUMENTS

1. What were Hitler's aims as expressed in the Hossbach memoir? How did he plan to achieve them?

2. What effect did Emperor Hirohito's broadcast have on the Japanese?

3. How did the American and Soviet sides each perceive the Cuban missile crisis?

4. Why was Martin Luther King, Jr., "impatient" with the progress of African Americans in the United States?

TERM-PAPER TOPICS

The Road to Munich: Appeasement and Aggression
Hitler and Mussolini: The Brutal Friendship
The Genesis of the Nazi-Soviet Pact
The Attack on Pearl Harbor
India and the Second World War
Resistance Movements in Occupied Europe
From Torch to Overlord: The Politics of the Second Front
The Holocaust
The Decision to Drop the Atomic Bomb
The Founding of the United Nations
Victors' Justice: The Nuremberg and Tokyo War Crimes Tribunals
The Origins of the Cold War
The Marshall Plan and the Recovery of Europe
The Truman Doctrine and the Idea of Containment
The Formation of the Soviet Bloc
McCarthyism and the Crisis of American Liberalism
De-Stalinization and the Crisis of the Soviet Bloc
Varieties of Communism
The Turbulent Sixties: From Civil Rights to Vietnam
Women's Rights and Gay Liberation: The Forging of an Alliance
From Welfare State to Privatization: Crises of the Postwar Economy

CHAPTER 40

REVIVAL AND REVOLUTION IN EAST ASIA

OUTLINE

OVERVIEW

The postwar period saw profound transformations in the societies of East Asia. These included revolutions in China and Indochina, decolonization in Malaya, Indonesia, and the Philippines, the demilitarization and recovery of Japan, the division of Korea, and the establishment of thriving commercial economies in Taiwan, South Korea, Singapore, and Hong Kong.

China and Japan remained after the war, as before, the most significant presences in East Asia. Japan demonstrated remarkable adaptability, resourcefulness, and social cohesion in the aftermath of its defeat. With its cities devastated both by conventional and atomic bombing and its economy in ruins, it rapidly rebuilt under American occupation, aided in no small part by the desire of the United States to use it as a counterweight to Russian power in the Far East, and after 1949 against China as well. Its new, American-sponsored constitution gave it a modern parliamentary regime based on universal suffrage that remains a stable and effective partner of the business trusts that have traditionally dominated the economy. By refusing to rearm, the Japanese placed themselves under the American military umbrella and thereby reaped the benefits of having their defense costs shouldered by the United States. Japan's postwar position has been characterized by extraordinary economic success and political restraint, a combination that has afforded it the comforts of a great power with few of the risks.

With the end of World War II, Nationalist and Communist forces resumed their struggle for power in China; the former, despite American aid, were soon defeated, and evacuated to Taiwan. China thus embarked on a new phase of its long revolution, with the Communist leadership under Mao Tse-tung providing subsistence but little sustained growth while lurching through disastrous experiments in social engineering. The worst of these, the so-called Cultural Revolution, occurred in the 1960s when China was almost wholly isolated from the world after a war with the United States over Korea (1950-1953) and a bitter ideological rift with the Soviet Union. Recent turbulence, including the 1989 massacre of student protestors in Tienanmen Square, suggests that China's road to modernization will continue to be a difficult one for some time to come.

The most pervasive presence in postwar Asia has been the United States, which with the withdrawal of Britain and France remains the only significant Western power in the region. It has fought major wars in Korea and Indochina as well as waging counterinsurgency campaigns in Malaya, Indonesia, and the Philippines through local proxies; its forces remain in Japan, South Korea, and the Philippines, while military agreements tie it to Thailand, Australia, New Zealand, and Taiwan. In Japan, its influence has been positive, although the Philippines, which it granted independence in 1946, remains a client state. Its rivalry with the Communist bloc brought a devastating war to the Korean peninsula, the legacy of which remains a divided country. Most disastrous was its attempt to replace the French in Indochina, which resulted in the first unequivocal defeat in American military history, and wreaked both destruction and political chaos on the people of Vietnam, Laos, and Cambodia. Nonetheless, as the student protest movement in China has shown, the American ideal can inspire great fervor, even if the American presence does not.

Socially, much has changed in postwar Asia. Legislation protecting women and granting them legal equality has been enacted throughout the region, while the pressures of an expanding marketplace have even more directly affected them. Nonetheless, traditional patterns of subordination remain deeply ingrained even in a fully industrialized society such as Japan, while in China, attempts to mobilize labor and control population growth, combined with the patrilocal family system, have placed great pressure on women.

East Asia's rapid economic growth—greater since World War II than that of any other region—has been accompanied by rapid urbanization, industrial pollution, and environmental depletion. These problems are similar to those that attended Western industrialization, but on a larger scale and in an ecologically more sensitive setting.

POINTS TO PONDER

1. East Asia has undergone radical political and economic change since World War II.

2. Much of the region's instability in the postwar period has resulted from Communist revolutions and insurgencies, invariably resisted by the United States.

3. The United States remains the only significant Western power in Asia, where it is a major economic, political, and military presence.

4. East Asia's rapid economic development has resulted in growing prosperity but also severe social and ecological strains.

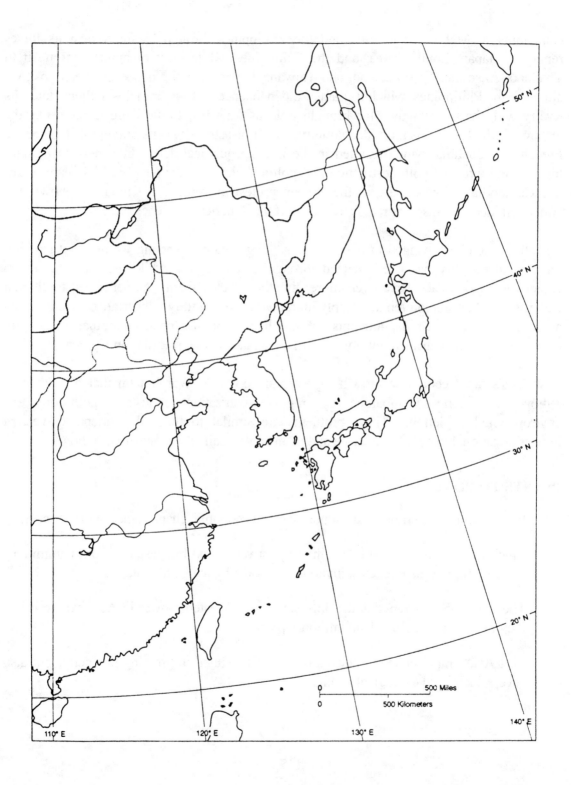

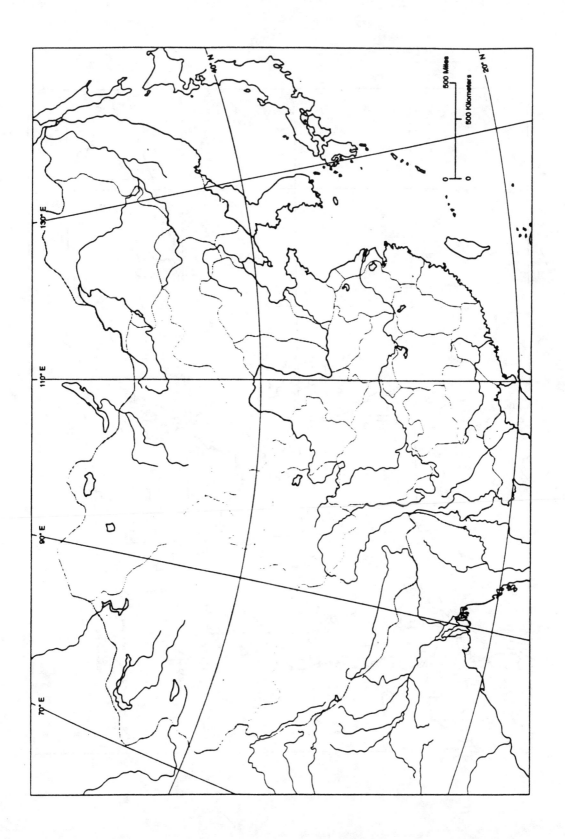

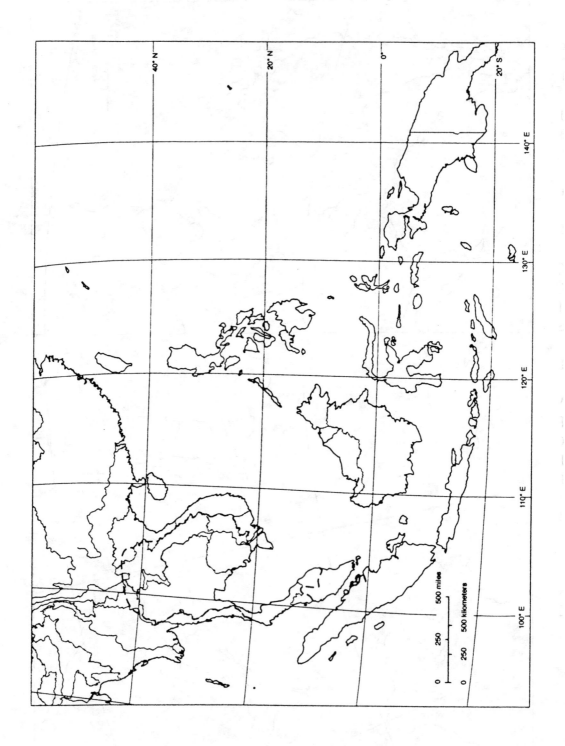

GEOGRAPHY

Locate the following on the first map:

Japan	North Korea
Tokyo	Pyongyang
Kyoto	South Korea
Osaka	Seoul
Hiroshima	Nagasaki

Locate the following on the second map:

China	Taiwan
Outer Mongolia	Hong Kong
Tibet	Canton
Shanghai	Peking (Beijing)

Locate the following on the third map:

Vietnam	Hanoi
Ho Chi Minh City (Saigon)	Laos
Cambodia	Thailand
Indonesia	Philippines
Manila	Singapore

1. How did the success of the Chinese Communist revolution affect the geographical balance of Southeast Asia?

2. How does the map of China reflect its relative population distribution?

CHRONOLOGY

Number the following in correct chronological sequence:

1. _____ Tet Offensive

2. _____ Student occupation of Tienanmen Square

3. _____ Great Leap Forward in China

4. _____ Counterinsurgency campaign in Indonesia

5. _____ Marcos dictatorship falls

6. _____ Armistice in Korea

7. _____ Paris Accords

8. _____ Pol Pot regime in Cambodia

9. _____ American occupation of Japan ends

IDENTIFICATION

1. Douglas MacArthur

2. Mao Tse-tung

3. Chou En-lai

4. *Little Red Book*

5. Gang of Four

6. 38th Parallel

7. Geneva Conference

8. National Liberation Front

9. Ho Chi Minh

10. Corazon Aquino

11. Achmed Sukarno

12. Khmer Rouge

13. Ne Win

14. Teng Hsiao-p'ing (Deng Xiaoping)

15. Tienanmen Square massacre

DEFINITION

1. American occupation

2. Mass Line

3. Revisionism

4. Cultural Revolution

5. Red Guards

6. Nixon shock

7. Guided democracy

8. Domino theory

COMPLETION

1. The growth rate of _____ between 1950 and 1975 was greater than that ever measured for any country in a comparable period of time.

2. An American mission led by _____ tried unsuccessfully to mediate between Nationalist and Communist forces after World War II.

3. Mao's Great Leap Forward led to mass _____.

4. In an attempt to control population, China after 1983 penalized families for having more than _____.

5. When _____ advocated attacking Chinese bases and using atomic weapons during the Korean War, he was removed from command by _____.

6. The French position in Vietnam became untenable after their defeat at _____.

7. The U.S. Congress gave President Johnson power to act militarily in Vietnam by the

    _____.

8. The Communist dictator responsible for the deaths of perhaps a third of Cambodia's

    people was _____.

9. Chinese women were given the right to choose their husbands freely for the first time

    by _____.

10. In large parts of Southeast Asia, _____ is being

    depleted to supply lumber.

SHORT ANSWER

1. What major changes were brought about in Japanese society by the American
    occupation?

2. How did Japan respond to American efforts to rearm it?

3. Why was Korea divided in 1945?

4. What differences of politics and ideology led to the Sino-Soviet split?

5. What was the effect of the Cultural Revolution on Chinese life?

6. How has China attempted to steer a different course since the death of Mao Tse-tung?

7. How has the United States asserted itself as a Pacific power since World War II?

8. Why was the United States unable to prevail in Vietnam despite overwhelmingly superior firepower?

9. How has the status of women in East Asia changed since the end of World War II?

10. What problems have economic modernization presented to East Asia?

UNDERSTANDING THE DOCUMENTS

1. What does the description of MacArthur suggest about his character?

2. How do the exchanges between Mao's Chinese defenders and his Soviet critics reveal the struggle for revolutionary supremacy between the two groups?

3. What is Mao's view of the people? How does he regard revolution itself?

TERM-PAPER TOPICS

After the Bomb: The Cultural Effects of Nuclear Devastation in Japan
The American Occupation of Japan
Tokyo: From Shogunal Citadel to World Capital
The Rise of Japanese Feminism
Asian Colossus: The Postwar Economy of Japan
The Chinese Civil War
The Sino-Soviet Split
The Cultural Revolution
After Mao: Making the New China
Rebellion and Repression: The Student Movement for Democracy in China
Women and the Family in Contemporary China
Korea: A Nation Divided
The Vietnam War and American Opinion
The Killing Field: Cambodia Under the Khmer Rouge
The Philippines: Democracy or Dependency?
Development and Ecology in Contemporary East Asia

CHAPTER 41

NATIONALISM AND REVOLUTION: INDIA, PAKISTAN, IRAN, AND THE MIDDLE EAST

OUTLINE

OVERVIEW

The long arc of states that extends westward from the Bay of Bengal to the Gulf of Tripoli is home to most of the world's Muslims, and the center of the holiest places of the Islamic faith. It is also a region shared by three other world religions, Hinduism, Judaism, and Christianity. The often violent interaction both between and within these faiths has been a major element of postwar history.

In India, religious animosity between Hindu and Muslim, fanned by personal rivalry among the country's political leadership, led to its division at independence into the states of India and Pakistan, and a massive population transfer amid chaos and violence. In the Middle East, the founding of the Jewish state of Israel in 1948 has polarized politics for more than four decades, with conflict spilling directly or indirectly into every state of the area. Israel itself, with the territories it has occupied since 1967, is the prime locus of the conflict, but it has taken an even heavier toll in Lebanon, where a civil war has raged since 1975. In addition, violence has erupted between a revived Shi'ite fundamentalism and the Sunni majority within Islam itself, most recently expressed in the bitter war between Iran and Iraq and the civil war in Algeria.

Almost every state in the arc has been created, liberated, or revolutionized in the period since World War I, and not infrequently all three. Decolonization resulted in the creation of India and Pakistan; from the latter was carved a new entity, Bangladesh. Egypt and Syria regained their ancient independence from Britain and France respectively, and Iran violently repudiated Western influence in 1979. States such as Saudi Arabia were created by enterprising rulers, whereas others, such as Jordan, were the product of political compromise. The creation of Israel by dedicated Zionists following the Holocaust in Europe was perhaps the most extraordinary and certainly the most controversial foundation in the region; tragically, it represents both a dream achieved and a dream denied, that of Palestinian Arab nationalism. Nowhere in the world today is nationalism so volatile, or so dangerously mixed with religion.

The entire region has also been an arena of great power competition. Up to the end of World War II, British and French interests predominated; with their withdrawal, the United States and the Soviet Union jockeyed for influence. Focused for almost two decades around Israel and Egypt, it was most recently played out in the Afghan War, and given Russia's traditional strategic interests in the region as well as the Western stake in Mideast oil, it seems likely to persist in one form or another. The united international response to Saddam Hussein's seizure of Kuwait in 1990 may prove an exceptional event, although American influence in the region is clearly predominant at the moment.

No area of the world has changed complexion more frequently or rapidly than the Muslim arc. Desert kingdoms have risen to world prominence and almost as suddenly faded; the OPEC cartel, which once seemed to hold the balance of the world's industrial economy in its hands, has lost much of its commanding position within a few years. The only constant has remained the bitter Arab-Israeli conflict, and the communal violence that, from Lebanon to Sri Lanka, continues to divide the region. Yet the overall success of the world's largest democracy, India, remains as well as a testimony of the ability of new nations to build a stable political culture amid religious and political diversity.

POINTS TO PONDER

1. Most of the world's Muslims live in newly formed or reformed states along an arc from the Bay of Bengal to the Gulf of Tripoli.

2. Tension and violence has marked the postwar history of the region, most persistently in the Arab-Israeli conflict.

3. The superpowers actively competed for influence in the region until the collapse of the USSR.

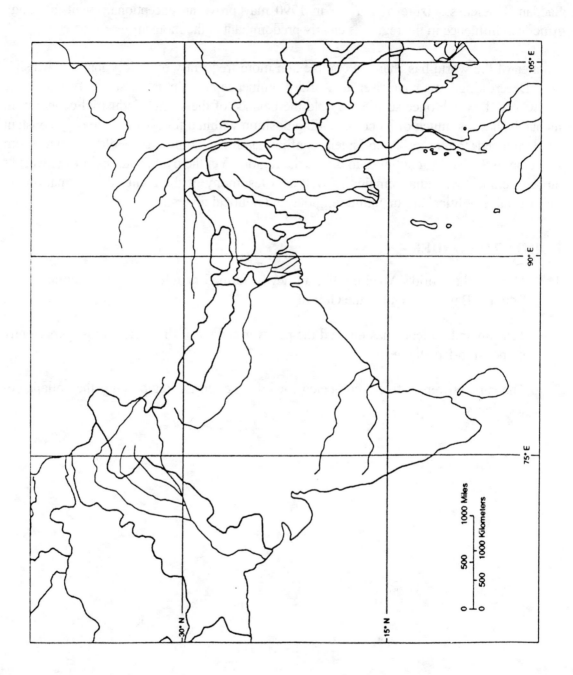

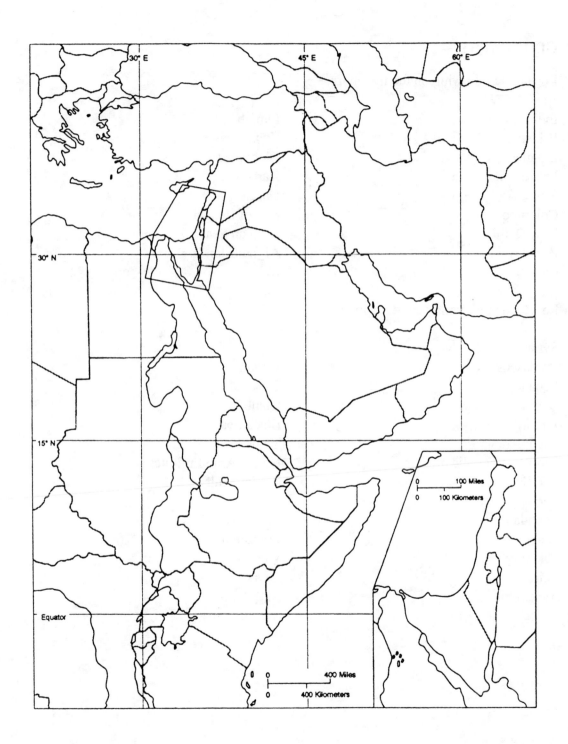

30° E 45° E 60° E

30° N

15° N

Equator

100 Miles
100 Kilometers

400 Miles
400 Kilometers

GEOGRAPHY

Locate the following on the first map:

India	Punjab
Pakistan	Kashmir
Bangladesh	Islamabad
Palk Strait	Karachi
Sri Lanka	Dacca
Colombo	Bay of Bengal
New Delhi	Arabian Sea
Bombay	Afghanistan
Calcutta	Kabul

Locate the following on the second map:

Syria	Libya
Damascus	Tripoli
Lebanon	Turkey
Beirut	Istanbul
Jordan	Black Sea
Saudi Arabia	Yemen
People's Republic of Yemen	United Arab Emirates
Red Sea	Persian Gulf
Iraq	Iran
Baghdad	Teheran
Israel	Jerusalem
Tel Aviv	West Bank
Cairo	Egypt
Alexandria	Nile River

1. Why does the Muslim arc's location make it a matter of significant concern to Russia and China?

2. Why is Iran's position of such strategic importance to the whole of the Muslim arc?

CHRONOLOGY

Number the following in correct chronological sequence:

1. _____ Nasser seizes control of the Suez Canal

2. _____ Assassination of Mahatma Gandhi

3. _____ Israel invades Lebanon

4. _____ Khomeini takes power in Iran

5. _____ Chinese-Indian border war

6. _____ Bangladesh becomes a state

7. _____ Six Day War

8. _____ Benazir Bhutto becomes President of Pakistan

9. _____ Camp David Accords

IDENTIFICATION

1.   Kashmir Conflict

2.   Indira Gandhi

3.   Sikhs

4.   Zulfikar Ali Bhutto

5.   Palestine

6.   Dome of the Rock

7.   Neguib Azouri

8.   Ibn–Saud

9.   David Ben–Gurion

10.   Gamal Abdel Nasser

11.   League of Arab States

12.   Baghdad Pact

13.   Muhammad Mossadegh

14.   Yom Kippur War

15.   Yasir Arafat

DEFINITION

1.   White Revolution

2.   Partition of Palestine

3.   Shuttle diplomacy

4. Ba'ath movement

5. *Histadrut*

6. *Chadar*

7. *Intifada*

8. *Jihad*

COMPLETION

1. The Indian Muslim leader responsible for the creation of Pakistan was

    _____.

2. The first prime minister of independent India was _____

    _____.

3. The contending population groups of Sri Lanka are the _____ and

    the _____.

4. At the end of World War II, the paramount power in the Middle East was

   _____.

5. The city sacred to three world religions is _____.

6. The major construction project of the Nasser years in Egypt was the

   _____.

7. The short-lived political union between Egypt and Syria was known as

   _____ _____.

8. The first Islamic state to replace the Koranic family law with a civil code was

   _____.

9. The reigning dynasty in Iran prior to the Islamic Revolution of 1979 was the

   _____ family.

10. The Gulf War was precipitated by Iraq's seizure of _____.

SHORT ANSWER

1. Why was British India partitioned at independence?

2. Why did Indira Gandhi declare a state of national emergency? What was the result?

267

3. What circumstances led to the secession of East Pakistan as the new nation of Bangladesh?

4. Why did the Arab League reject the partition of Palestine?

5. Why has the state of Israel been unable to define what constitutes a Jew?

6. What were the circumstances under which the Palestine Liberation Organization was organized?

7. Why did the Camp David Accords fail to produce a lasting settlement of the Arab-Israeli conflict?

8. What were the domestic goals of Nasser's revolution in Egypt? How successful was he in achieving them?

9. How did OPEC use its oil monopoly in an attempt to achieve political goals?

10. Why was Khomeini's Islamic Revolution successful in toppling the regime of the Shah in Iran?

UNDERSTANDING THE DOCUMENTS

1. How did Jinnah and Nehru differ in their vision of the coming independence of British India?

2. How does Nehru attempt to define India's place in the world?

3. How do the Israeli and Palestinian statements express opposed views of their religious and territorial claims?

4. How does the Ayatollah Khomeini express his rejection of Western values? How does he propose to "liberate" Islamic women from them?

TERM-PAPER TOPICS

Mahatma Gandhi: Father of Indian Independence

Problems of Indian Democracy

Three Women Leaders of Modern Asia: Indira Gandhi, Sirimavo Bandaranaike,
    Benazir Bhutto

Pakistan Between the Great Powers

Sri Lanka: A Land Divided

The Afghan War: Russia's Vietnam

Islamic Fundamentalism and the Role of Women

Arab Socialism and the Politics of Oil

Nasser and the Modern Arab World

Khomeini and His Revolution

The Revival of Islamic Fundamentalism

Lebanon: The Collapse of a Nation

Ben–Gurion and the Establishment of Israel

Israel and the Arab World

The Palestinian Nationalist Movement

The Gulf War and Its Aftermath

CHAPTER 42

DECOLONIZATION AND DEVELOPMENT: AFRICA AND LATIN AMERICA

OUTLINE

OVERVIEW

Africa and Latin America present contrasting studies in development. Both have faced a difficult colonial legacy and continuing dependence on the advanced industrial states together with rising populations, persistent poverty and inequity, and political instability. The circumstances of each have varied widely however, and each contains a diversity of populations, languages, and cultures.

Africa, colonized for centuries but controlled for only about 75 years, regained its independence after 1945. Though brief, European domination had a profound impact; apart from the millions of black Africans who died in the Belgian Congo, tribal boundaries, laws, and customs were erased everywhere, and the nations that emerged from the postwar period—for the most part peacefully, but with significant exceptions in Algeria, Kenya, Zaire, Zimbabwe, and Angola—were often imperial composites with little ethnic unity and disputed frontiers. The result was civil war, as in Nigeria, the Sudan, Burundi, Uganda, and Somalia, and a typical pattern of one-party dictatorships. Statesmen of vision, such as Jomo Kenyatta in Kenya and Julius Nyerere in Tanzania, proved capable of creating genuine nationhood, but elsewhere violence and corruption was too often the rule. In South Africa, a black majority government under Nelson Mandela took power in 1994 after decades of white supremacist rule.

Latin American independence came much earlier, between 1810 and 1825, but with it too came the Monroe Doctrine, and the overwhelming shadow the United States has cast on the region since 1898. As in the case of Africa, nations emerged with shallow roots and unsettled borders. Few of them achieved stability or successful civilian democracy. The pattern of caudillism in Latin America, tied to military and comprador (collaborationist) elites subsidized by the United States, thus offers a parallel to the dictatorial regimes of Africa. Civilian rule at military sufferance alternating with junta regimes has become a recurrent feature in much of South America, including Bolivia, Peru, Chile, Argentina, and Brazil. Much of the region's economy has now become involved in supplying the U.S. drug market, including Colombia, Bolivia, Peru, and virtually all of Central America. Generally, the United States remains the largest single influence in the political and economic destiny of virtually every Latin American state.

The United States intervened directly to suppress leftist regimes in Guatemala, the Dominican Republic, and Chile in the postwar period, after previously occupying Haiti and Nicaragua for lengthy periods. Nonetheless, two such regimes emerged, in Cuba under Fidel Castro and, for a decade, in Nicaragua under the Sandinistas. Both states sought Soviet assistance, bringing the Cold War to Latin America as struggles in Ethiopia, Angola, Mozambique, and Namibia brought it to Africa. The collapse of the Soviet Union, here as elsewhere, led to settlements favorable to the United States, as the Sandinistas were voted out of office after a prolonged U.S.-sponsored insurrection, and rebels in El Salvador reached an accommodation with the U.S.-supported government. Only an isolated Cuba remained defiant in the 1990s.

POINTS TO PONDER

1. Africa and Latin America have both experienced difficulties in development based in part on the legacy of former colonial regimes.

2. Arbitrary colonial boundaries have left many new African states with tribal instability and disputed frontiers.

3. The United States is the most dominant single influence in Latin America.

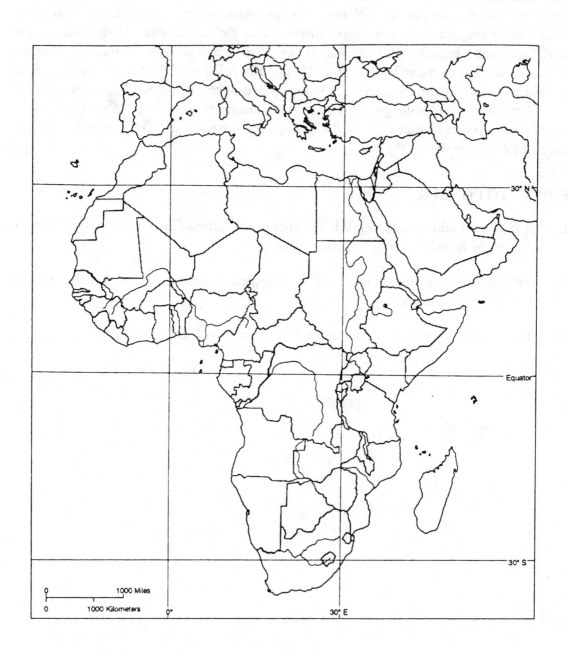

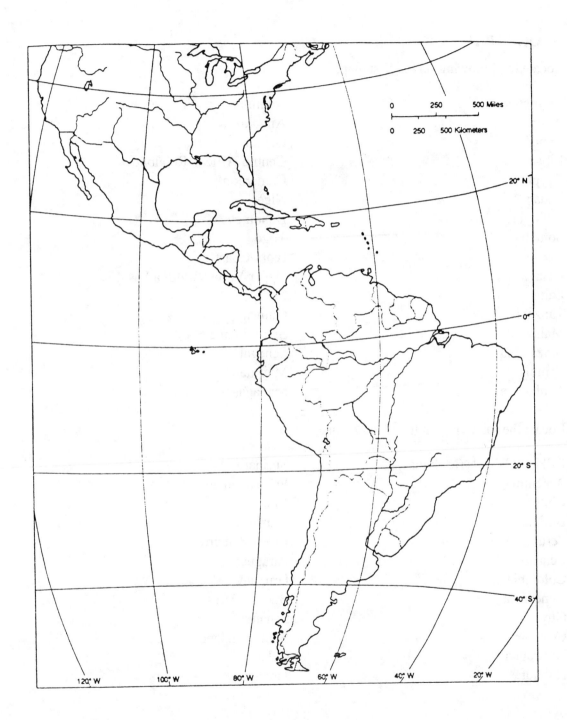

500 Miles

500 Kilometers

20° N

0°

20° S

40° S

120° W   100° W   80° W   60° W   40° W   20° W

GEOGRAPHY

Locate the following on the first map:

Morocco	Namibia
Algeria	Angola
Tunisia	Gabon
Libya	Central African Republic
Egypt	Cameroon
Sudan	Nigeria
Ethiopia	Dahomey
Somalia	Togo
Kenya	Ivory Coast
Uganda	Upper Volta (Burkina Faso)
Zaire	Mali
Tanzania	Guinea
Malawi	Sierra Leone
Mozambique	Senegal
Zambia	Mauritania
Zimbabwe	Madagascar

Locate the following on the second map:

Falkland Islands (Malvinas)	Suriname
Argentina	French Guiana
Chile	Brazil
Bolivia	Brasilia
Peru	Rio de Janeiro
Ecuador	Paraguay
Colombia	Uruguay
Venezuela	Buenos Aires
Guyana	Panama
Costa Rica	Bahama Islands
Nicaragua	Cuba
Honduras	Jamaica

El Salvador

Guatemala

Belize

Mexico

Gulf of Mexico

Miami

Haiti

Dominican Republic

Puerto Rico

Virgin Islands

Grenada

Trinidad

1. Where are the major disputed frontiers in Africa and Latin America?

2. Why have land-use patterns in Africa and Latin America become a matter of world concern?

CHRONOLOGY

Number the following in correct chronological sequence:

1. _____ Castro seizes power in Cuba

2. _____ Ibo rebels declare state of Biafra

3. _____ Algeria wins independence from France

4. _____ Nelson Mandela elected president of South Africa

5. _____ Overthrow of Allende government in Chile

6. _____ Founding of the African National Congress

7. _____ Falklands War

8. _____ Mexican republic established

9. _____ Organization of African Unity formed

IDENTIFICATION

1. Marcus Garvey

2. Julius Nyerere

3. Jomo Kenyatta

4. Nelson Mandela

5. FLN

6. Sahel

7. Big Bush

8. Juan Perón

9. Sendero Luminoso

10. Gran Chaco War

11. United Fruit Company

12. Che Guevara

13. Porfirio Díaz

14. Gabriel Garcia Marquez

15. Victor Paz Estenssoro

DEFINITION

1. West African National Congress

2. *Apartheid*

3. *Caudillo*

4.   *Machismo*

5.   Liberation Theology

6.   Monroe Doctrine

7.   Sandinistas

8.   "Mothers of the disappeared"

COMPLETION

1.   _____ was the mineral-rich province that attempted to secede from the

Congo at independence.

2.   _____ is the South African clergyman who received the Nobel

Prize for his work on behalf of his black countrymen.

3.   The first President of Ghana was _____.

4. The secret terrorist society sworn to drive all white settlers out of Kenya was the

    _____.

5. The Africa state where Islamic fundamentalism has taken deepest root is

    _____.

6. The dominant progressive force in Peru between 1924 and 1968 was the organization

    known as _____.

7. The mixed Spanish and Indian population of Latin America is called

    _____.

8. The largest Jewish community in Latin America resides in _____.

9. The first Latin American nation to win independence was _____.

10. The last Latin American nation to grant women the right to vote was _____.

SHORT ANSWER

1. Why did France resist granting independence to Algeria?

2. Why did Nigeria's tribal conflicts lead it to civil war?

3. Why did Belgium's abrupt withdrawal from the Congo produce chaos?

4.   How was Jomo Kenyatta able to forge unity in Kenya?

5.   Why did the white South African regime negotiate a peaceful transfer of power to the nonwhite majority?

6.   Why has Peronism proved an enduring force in Argentina?

7.   Why did the United States sponsor the military coup against the Allende government in Chile?

8.   How has excessive reliance on a single cash crop affected Latin American nations?

9.   What were the common factors behind the leftist revolutions in Cuba and Nicaragua?

10.   Why is the Roman Catholic hierarchy frequently at odds with the local clergy in Latin America?

UNDERSTANDING THE DOCUMENTS

1. Why does Kawawa reject the idea of a non–racial society in Africa?

2. What effect has apartheid had on black proletarian families in South Africa?

3. What are the chief elements of Peronism as expressed by Eva Perón?

4. How does Che Guevara depart from the traditional Leninist strategy for revolution? In which respects is he closer to the ideas of Mao?

TERM-PAPER TOPICS

Negritude and the Growth of Black Consciousness in Africa
Algeria and the Crisis of French Decolonization
Superpower Rivalries in Postcolonial Africa
The Nigerian Civil War: Causes and Consequences
The Sahel: Manmade Disaster
Jomo Kenyatta and the Making of Kenya
The Triumph of Black Majority Rule in South Africa
Ethnic Conflict in Africa: The Dilemma of a Continent
The Problem of Land Reform in Latin America
Perón and Peronism
The United States and the Latin American Military
Brazil: The Troubled Giant
Drugs and Dollars: Issues and Alternatives in Latin America
Church and State in Latin America
Cuba and the Latin American Community
Feminism and Machismo in Latin America

GLOBAL ESSAY

MAPS AND THEIR MAKERS (II)

OVERVIEW

The voyages of Columbus and his successors made a true map of the world possible for the first time, while increasingly accurate maps—especially after Mercator's projections had enabled cartographers to represent the three-dimensional globe on a two-dimensional surface—facilitated the work of explorers, merchants, missionaries, and conquerors. The new knowledge of the terrestrial world stimulated speculation about the heavens as well, and with Galileo's discovery of Jupiter's moons it was clear that the heavens too would have to be remapped.

The Atlantic seaboard was reliably mapped in the seventeenth and eighteenth centuries, but it was not until the Lewis and Clark expedition of 1804-1806 that the true dimensions of North America were revealed. Captain Cook's expeditions mapped the northwest American coastline and virtually all of the Pacific, and Australia was demonstrated to be a continent in 1801. Asia and Africa were mapped in the course of Europe's colonial expansion in the nineteenth century. The last of the continents to be surveyed, Antarctica, did not begin to yield its secrets until the twentieth century. At the same time, the oceans were sounded and mapped, revealing a planet beneath the planet, with topographic features larger than any to be found on the surface.

Although the Copernican theory required a larger celestial sphere than Ptolemy's and though Giordano Bruno had argued for an infinite universe as early as the sixteenth century, it was only with Herschel's galactic hypothesis that the immense magnitude of the universe, if not its true scale, could be appreciated. The development of radio telescopy in the twentieth century and the discovery of quasars suggests now that light propagated before the existence of our planet has now reached the Earth.

IDENTIFICATION

1. Gerardus Mercator

2. Prime meridian

3. Northwest Passage

4. Terra Australis

5. United States Geologic Survey

6. Continental drift

7. Hubble's law

8. Quasars

COMPLETION

1. The first atlas was Ortelius' _____.

2. Newton proved that there was no difference between celestial and terrestrial mechanics in his _____.

3. An international conference established _____ as the prime meridian in 1884.

4. The _____, a complex device consisting of telescopes, reflectors, and angle registers, was developed in the eighteenth century to measure distance.

5. The geologist _____ refuted the idea that the earth was only a few thousand years old.

6. The belief in intelligent life on Mars was based on the apparent sighting of _____ on the planet's surface.

7. The largest topographic feature of the Earth is _____.

8. The existence of other galaxies was proved by _____.

SHORT ANSWER

1. Why did Galileo's discovery of Jupiter's moons stimulate interest in the heavens?

2. How did cartography become a weapon in the struggle for empire?

3. Why was the fact that the earth is not a perfect sphere of practical importance?

4. How did Matteo Ricci seek to flatter the Chinese emperor with his world map?

5. Why were Americans panicked by the radio hoax that announced the landing of Martians?

6. How has the theory of "continental drift" altered our perception of the earth's evolution?

7. For what important purposes are maps used today?

TERM-PAPER TOPICS

The First Printed Maps
The Impact of Galileo's Discoveries
Science Fiction of the Seventeenth Century
Cartography and the Quest for Empire
The Search for the Northwest Passage
John Wesley Powell: Cartographer of the American West
Mapping the World's Oceans
Radio Astronomy: Mapping the Last Frontier

CHAPTER 43

THE CONTEMPORARY AGE

OUTLINE

OVERVIEW

The Cuban missile crisis was soon followed by the assassination of President John F. Kennedy and the removal of Prime Minister Nikita Khrushchev. Under a succession of American presidents and, in the Soviet Union, the long dominance of Leonid Brezhnev (1964-1982), Soviet-American relations evolved toward joint rule (a condominium) based on the mutual recognition of established frontiers and interests and a series of agreements, beginning with the Limited Test Ban Treaty, designed to stabilize if not curtail the arms race. Thus the United States was able to pursue its ill-fated war in Vietnam (1965-1975) and the Soviet Union its equally catastrophic venture in Afghanistan (1979-1989) without overt interference from its fellow superpower.

Despite vigorous American efforts to contain the perceived Sino-Soviet colossus that physically dominated most of Eurasia by means of regional military alliances, many newly independent states, notably Egypt, India, and Indonesia, remained nonaligned, sometimes forming their own associations (such as the Organization of African Unity) or cartels (of which the most successful was the Organization of Petroleum Exporting Countries, or OPEC). western Europe too began to reassert its independence; in 1957, six European states organized the Common Market, designed to integrate the continent into a single economic and ultimately political union. Charles de Gaulle led France out of NATO, and West German Chancellor Willy Brandt moved to improve relations with the Communist East. By 1987, Western Europe had become the world's largest commercial unit, although impediments to fuller unity remained.

The Cold War was briefly revived, at least on a rhetorical level, during the presidency of Ronald Reagan (1981-1989), but the accession of Mikhail Gorbachev to power in the Soviet Union in 1985 brought about a rapid liberalization and a deescalation of tensions. Proclaiming a fundamental restructuring of the Soviet Union as his goal, Gorbachev instituted limited market reforms and invited open criticism of the Soviet regime. The unlooked-for result was the collapse of Soviet power in eastern Europe in 1989, the reunification of Germany in 1990, and the breakup of the Soviet Union itself in 1991. Conflicts flared among several of the successor states, the former Yugoslavia broke apart amidst civil war in 1992, and the Czechoslovak union was peacefully dissolved in 1993. Health and living standards in the region plummeted, particularly in Russia itself, the largest of the former Soviet republics and still geographically the largest state on the globe. The Western world meanwhile faced persistent economic stagnation, and its response to events, including the war in Bosnia, the largest conflict in Europe since World War II, remained halting and uncertain. Economically interdependent as never before, the world faced a new era of political instability that threatened to widen the gap between the developed and the developing world yet further.

POINTS TO PONDER

1. The first sustained relaxation of East-West tensions in the Cold War era followed the Cuban missile crisis.

2. Newly independent states in the developing world resisted incorporation into the East-West power blocs.

3. The collapse of the Soviet Union and its empire followed swiftly on the reforms instituted by Mikhail Gorbachev.

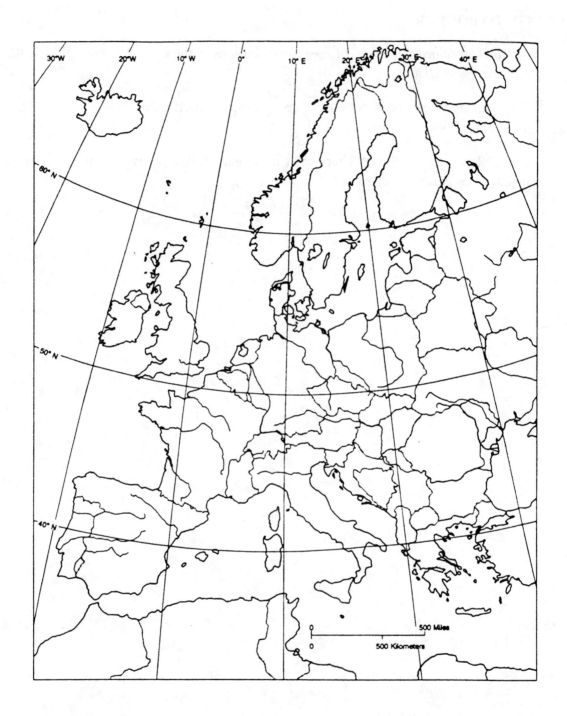

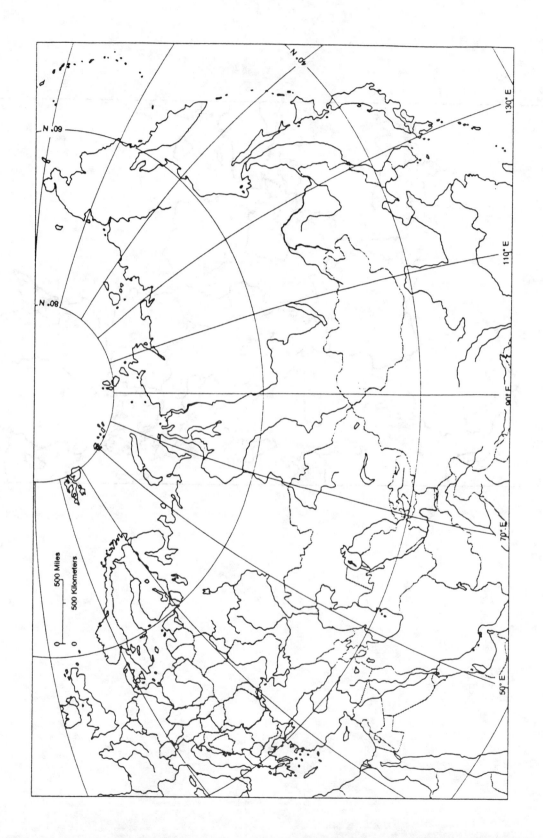

GEOGRAPHY

Locate the following on the first map:

Germany	Bulgaria
Poland	Romania
Slovak Republic	Former Yugoslavia
Czech Republic	Albania
Hungary	Greece
Moldova	

Locate the following on the second map:

Serbia	Croatia
Bosnia-Herzegovina	Slovenia
Macedonia	Montenegro

Locate the following on the third map:

Russia	Armenia
Moscow	Azerbaijan
Lithuania	Uzbekistan
Latvia	Turkmenistan
Estonia	Kazakhstan
Ukraine	Tajikistan
Georgia	Kyrgyzstan

CHRONOLOGY

Number the following in correct chronological sequence:

1. _____ Soviet invasion of Czechoslovakia

2. _____ Helsinki Accords

295

3. _____ Bandung Conference

4. _____ First Nuclear Test Ban Treaty

5. _____ Germany reunified

6. _____ Solidarity movement begins

7. _____ East European Communist regimes fall

8. _____ OPEC embargo

9. _____ Yeltsin invades Chechnya

IDENTIFICATION

1. Bandung Conference

2. Commonwealth of Independent States (CIS)

3. Organization of African Unity

4. Charles de Gaulle

5. OPEC

6. Single European Act

7. Slobodan Milosevic

8. "Star Wars"

9. Mikhail Gorbachev

10. Vaclav Havel

11. *Glasnost*

12. Watergate

13. Helsinki Accords

14. GATT

15. Brezhnev Doctrine

DEFINITION

1. Nonproliferation Treaty

2. Third Force

3. Common Market

4. Détente

COMPLETION

1. American involvement in the Vietnam War was officially ended with _____

    _____.

2. Western Communist parties espoused a policy of independence from both superpowers in the 1970s known as _____.

3. The collapse of the East German regime was precipitated by the destruction of

    _____.

4. Ethnic and religious conflict led to the outbreak of civil war in the former Communist state of _____ in the 1990s.

5. Antiballistic missiles (ABMs) were outlawed by _____.

6. Third World countries found a forum for their grievances during the Cold War in _____.

7. The collapse of Soviet Communism and the transformation of China into a market economy accelerated the growth of _____.

8. At the breakup of the Soviet Union, _____ became president of Russia.

9. The idea that fear of a devastating counterattack will inhibit nuclear war is called _____.

10. Mikhail Gorbachev's program to restructure Soviet society was called _____.

SHORT ANSWER

1. What factors contributed to the policy of détente between the superpowers?

2. How did nonaligned states attempt to resist pressure from the superpowers?

3. Why was Gorbachev unable to control the reforms he initiated in the Soviet Union?

4. To what extent was the movement toward disarmament successful?

5. What impact did economic developments in the Reagan period have on American foreign policy?

6. How did European efforts toward economic unity undermine American influence?

7. What steps have been taken to promote European economic unity?

8. Why did Soviet control of eastern Europe collapse?

9. Why did the Soviet Union collapse?

10. What were the causes of civil war in the former Yugoslavia?

UNDERSTANDING THE DOCUMENTS

1. How did Henry Kissinger interpret the meaning of détente?

2. How does Gorbachev invoke Leninist idealism in his vision of *perestroika*? To what tendencies in Soviet society does he oppose it?

3. Why does Vaclav Havel feel that the collapse of Communism in Europe signifies the end of an intellectual as well as a political era?

TERM-PAPER TOPICS

Détente and the Politics of Superpower Condominium
Third World Nonalignment and the Cold War
OPEC and the Politics of Oil
The Common Market and the Formation of a United Europe
Vietnam and the Limits of American Power
1989: Year of Revolution
The Gorbachev Revolution and the Fall of the Soviet Union
After Communism: Ethnic Conflict in Eastern Europe and the Commonwealth of
     Independent States
The Nuclear Dilemma: Proliferation and Arms Control After the Superpowers
The New Framework of Global Capitalism

EPILOGUE

OVERVIEW

The modern Western concept of secular progress, typified in Edward Bellamy's *Looking Backward*, departs from the vision of most other world cultures and from most of the Western experience as well. It is based in large degree on the identification of progress with material enhancement, which in turn rests on the ethos of liberal capitalism. Marxism, while challenging the mechanism of capitalism, has retained the optimism of liberal assumptions.

For many non-Western societies, the imposition of Western forms and standards by nineteenth-century imperialism meant severe cultural dislocation. Western-style technology and industrialization has been rejected by Third World leaders from Gandhi to Khomeini, while the experience of fascism, depression, and totalitarianism in the West itself has sobered the vision of progress. Our common heritage is made up of many separate traditions; no single vision can determine it. Rather, we must forge our common future from multiple perspectives, from respect for our diversity as well as hope for our unity, and with the faith not in a preordained utopia but in the power of freedom to create new value.

IDENTIFICATION

1. Edward Bellamy

2. *Brave New World*

3. George Orwell

DEFINITION

1. Progress

2. Modernization

3. Appropriate technology

4. Greenhouse effect

COMPLETION

1. The utopian tradition in Western thought stretches back to _____.

2. Indian conceptions of history have been _____.

3. In Hindu religion, humans aspire to _____, a spiritual state divorced from the material world.

4. The materialist theory of progress provided a rationale for _____.

5. India's struggle for independence from Western control was symbolized by _____ _____.

6. President John F. Kennedy's program of aid to Latin America was called

_____.

7. Western technology has often proved inappropriate for developing nations because of

its _____.

8. The dangers of nuclear power have been most recently demonstrated by the disaster at

the Soviet plant in _____.

SHORT ANSWER

1. How does Bellamy's *Looking Backward* reflect a belief in the inevitability of progress?

2. How is the concept of progress tied to the belief in natural economic laws?

3. What assumptions did Marxist reformers share with liberal capitalists?

4. What consequences did Huxley and Orwell fear from a technological society?

5. Why has Western-style modernization proved inappropriate to many developing societies?

6.	How has aid to underdeveloped nations often perpetuated forms of political and economic dependency?

7.	What are the major problems posed by present-day development?

TERM-PAPER TOPICS

The Concept of Secular Progress in the West
Marx's Vision of History
Critics of Progress: The Anti-Utopian Novel in the Twentieth Century
Indian Theories of History
Gandhi and the Resistance to Technology
The Islamic Revolution and the West
Aid and Dependency in the Third World
Implementing Appropriate Technology

ANSWERS

CHAPTER 21

Chronology

1. 4
2. 3
3. 1
4. 6
5. 2
6. 5
7. 7

Completion

1. Mediterranean, Indian Ocean
2. *jonya* system
3. Ethiopia
4. Sonni Ali
5. gender
6. Berbers
7. *signares*
8. Christian
9. Swahili
10. Great Zimbabwe
11. Asante, Dahomey

CHAPTER 22

Chronology

1. 4
2. 3
3. 7
4. 1
5. 2
6. 5
7. 6

Completion

1. Hung-wu
2. tributary
3. Cheng Ho (Zhengho)
4. cotton
5. Japan, Manila
6. Yung-lo (Yongluo)
7. *Water Margins, Golden Lotus*
8. tradition
9. Peking (Beijing)
10. Portuguese, Dutch
11. Inner Mongolia, Korea

CHAPTER 23

Completion

1. education (or learning)
2. ritual pollution, purity
3. estates
4. father
5. nuclear
6. divorce
7. the family
8. West Africa
9. procreation
10. Prussia
11. medreses
12. theft

CHAPTER 24

Chronology

1. 7
2. 1
3. 5
4. 4
5. 9
6. 6
7. 3
8. 2

Completion

1. Whigs and Tories
2. bureaucracy
3. Holy Synod
4. standing army
5. Madame de Maintenon
6. Hungary
7. Cavalier Parliament
9. France
10. the Great Elector

CHAPTER 25

Chronology

1. 4
2. 9
3. 3
4. 6
5. 1
6. 5
7. 2
8. 7
9. 8

Completion

1. Sir Francis Bacon
2. the telescope
3. the Arabs
4. Thomas Hobbes'
5. Mercator
6. Rene Descartes
7. *Don Quixote*
8. Aristarchus
9. Johann Sebastian Bach
10. gravity

CHAPTER 26

Chronology

1. 6
2. 2
3. 3
4. 5
5. 7
6. 1
7. 8
8. 9
9. 4

Completion

1. the Mediterranean
2. gold and silver bullion
3. Brazil
4. Liverpool
5. William Pitt the Elder
6. Quebec Act
7. Durham Report
8. free trade
9. James Madison
10. the Liberator

CHAPTER 27

Chronology

1. 4
2. 6
3. 7
4. 3
5. 9
6. 2
7. 5
8. 1
9. 8

Completion

1. John Locke
2. progress
3. Voltaire
4. property
5. Montesquieu
6. Frederick the Great
7. the Clapham sect
8. *Nathan the Wise*
9. Vienna
10. Joseph II

CHAPTER 28

Chronology

1. 4
2. 7
3. 1
4. 5
5. 8
6. 2
7. 9
8. 3
9. 6

Completion

1. the Estates General
2. Great Fear
3. Edmund Burke
4. bourgeoisie
5. Declaration of Pillnitz
6. federations
7. Jacobins (Montagnards); Girondins
8. *Levee en masse*
9. Napoleon Bonaparte
10. Trafalgar
11. Elba; St. Helena

GLOBAL ESSAY: DEATH AND THE HUMAN EXPERIENCE (II)

Completion

1. Munkar; Nakir
2. the soul leaves the body
3. Reformation; Bhakti movement
4. Muslims; Hindus
5. Huron Indians
6. nineteenth century
7. Jews
8. *Kiddush Hashem*

CHAPTER 29

Chronology

1. 3
2. 4
3. 9
4. 1
5. 6
6. 7
7. 8
8. 2
9. 5

Completion

1. Portuguese
2. Madras
3. Bengal
4. Sir William Jones
5. Calcutta
6. the Army of the Indus
7. Thomas Babington Macaulay
8. Bahadur Shah
9. the Ottoman Empire
10. Nadir Shah

CHAPTER 30

Chronology

1. 4
2. 1
3. 3
4. 7
5. 5
6. 2
7. 8
8. 6
9. 9

Completion

1. pure
2. the Americas
3. Kang Hsi
4. population
5. Canton
6. opium
7. *daimyos*
8. merchants
9. Kabuki
10. the emperor

CHAPTER 31

Chronology

1. 2
2. 6
3. 7
4. 3
5. 8
6. 9
7. 1
8. 4
9. 5

Completion

1. wood
2. pig iron; wrought iron
3. bourgeoisie
4. sixteen
5. *Essay on Population*
6. Robert Owen
7. sanitation
8. London
9. railroad
10. the United States

CHAPTER 32

Chronology

1. 3
2. 6
3. 4
4. 8
5. 2
6. 5
7. 1
8. 9
9. 7

Completion

1. Prussia
2. Troppau Protocol
3. Russia
4. Wordsworth; Coleridge
5. Hegel
6. *Liberty on the Barricades*; Delacroix
7. Saint-Simon
8. Karl Marx
9. Louis Kossuth
10. Piedmont

CHAPTER 33

Chronology

1. 5
2. 9
3. 1
4. 3
5. 8
6. 7
7. 6
8. 4
9. 2

Completion

1. nationalism
2. the Second Republic
3. plebiscites
4. Pius IX
5. Bismarck
6. *Realpolitik*
7. Ems Dispatch
8. the Magyars
9. intelligentsia
10. pogroms

CHAPTER 34

Chronology

1. 2
2. 4
3. 9
4. 1
5. 6
6. 8
7. 3
8. 7
9. 5

Completion

1. Queen Victoria
2. Liberals; Conservatives
3. Emile Zola
4. *Kulturkampf*
5. *Trasformismo*
6. the Generation of 1898
7. Social Darwinism
8. Mikhail Bakunin
9. the General Strike
10. Annie Besant; Charles Bradlaugh

GLOBAL ESSAY: WRITING AND COMMUNICATION (II)

1. tenth
2. Arab
3. the Reformation
4. revolutions
5. Ems Dispatch
6. photography
7. Africa
8. the Vietnam War

CHAPTER 35

Chronology

1. 5
2. 6
3. 7
4. 3
5. 2
6. 9
7. 4
8. 8
9. 1

Completion

1. Leopold II
2. Boers
3. Ethiopia
4. the Mutiny of 1857
5. Unequal treaties
6. Rice Christians
7. Korea
8. Manchuria
9. penal convicts
10. Indochina

CHAPTER 36

Chronology

1. 8
2. 3
3. 1
4. 2
5. 5
6. 9
7. 7
8. 4
9. 6

Completion

1. Hohenzollern Germany; Habsburg Austria-Hungary; Ottoman Turkey; Romanov Russia
2. the superman
3. Action Française
4. the Ring of the Nibelungen
5. Japan
6. blank check
7. League of Nations
8. Little Entente
9. *Lady Chatterley's Lover*
10. *The Decline of the West*

GLOBAL ESSAY: THE HUMAN IMAGE (II)

Completion

1. Medicis
2. Akbar
3. commercial society
4. Venus
5. Mannerists
6. *Death of Marat*
7. *The Scream*
8. pop art

CHAPTER 37

Chronology

1. 8
2. 3
3. 6
4. 4
5. 2
6. 5
7. 7
8. 9
9. 1

Completion

1. Nicholas II
2. Bolshevik; Menshevik
3. Joseph Stalin
4. warlords
5. Shanghai
6. Lu Hsun
7. Amritsar Massacre
8. *Ahimsa*
9. Faisal of Iraq
10. kibbutz

CHAPTER 38

Chronology

1. 8
2. 2
3. 7
4. 5
5. 6
6. 9
7. 1
8. 4
9. 3

Completion

1. capitalism; Communism
2. lower middle class
3. Kapp Putsch
4. *Mein Kampf*
5. Epic Theater
6. *tenentes*
7. the Nuremberg Laws
8. Jose Antonio Primo de Rivera
9. Sergei Kirov
10. the collapse of the New York Stock Exchange

CHAPTER 39

Chronology

1. 8
2. 2
3. 1
4. 4
5. 3
6. 9
7. 7
8. 5
9. 6

Completion

1. Ethiopia
2. the Axis
3. Munich Conference
4. Charles de Gaulle
5. the Manhattan Project
6. Potsdam
7. Nuremberg Tribunal
8. NATO
9. participatory democracy
10. revisionists

CHAPTER 40

Chronology

1. 5
2. 9
3. 3
4. 4
5. 8
6. 2
7. 6
8. 7
9. 1

Completion

1. Japan
2. George C. Marshall
3. starvation
4. one child
5. Douglas MacArthur; President Truman
6. Dien Bien Phu
7. Tongking Gulf Resolution
8. Pol Pot
9. the Marriage Law of 1950
10. tropical rain forest

CHAPTER 41

Chronology

1. 9
2. 8
3. 2
4. 3
5. 7
6. 5
7. 6
8. 1
9. 4

Completion

1. Ali Jinnah
2. Jawaharlal Nehru
3. Sinhalese; Tamils
4. Britain
5. Jerusalem
6. Aswan Dam
7. the United Arab Republic
8. Tunisia
9. Pahlavi
10. Kuwait

CHAPTER 42

Chronology

1. 3
2. 6
3. 4
4. 9
5. 7
6. 1
7. 8
8. 2
9. 5

Completion

1. Katanga
2. Desmond Tutu
3. Kwame Nkrumah
4. Mau Mau
5. Libya
6. APRA
7. *mestizo*
8. Argentina
9. Haiti
10. Paraguay

GLOBAL ESSAY: MAPS AND THEIR MAKERS (II)

Completion

1. Theater of the World
2. Principia Mathematica
3. Greenwich
4. Theodolite
5. James Hutton
6. canals
7. Mid-Ocean Ridge
8. Edwin Hubble

CHAPTER 43

Chronology

1. 3
2. 5
3. 1
4. 2
5. 8
6. 6
7. 7
8. 4
9. 9

Completion

1. the Paris Accords
2. Eurocommunism
3. the Berlin Wall
4. Yugoslavia
5. the SALT I Treaty
6. the United Nations
7. global capitalism
8. Boris Yeltsin
9. deterrence
10. *perestroika*

EPILOGUE

Completion

1. Plato's *Republic*
2. cyclical
3. nirvana
4. imperialism
5. the spinning wheel
6. the Alliance for Progress
7. large-scale character
8. Chernobyl